How to Get to the Top
Without Working Too Hard

HOW TO GET TO THE TOP

Without Working Too Hard

The ~~MBA~~ MCA for the real world of business

DICK LANNISTER

Matador
9 Priory Business Park
Kibworth Beauchamp
Leicestershire LE8 0RX, UK
Tel: 0116 279 2299
Email: books@troubador.co.uk
Web: www.troubador.co.uk/matador

ISBN 9781784623104

Disclaimer: This work is entirely fictitious. Any resemblance to real persons,
companies or organisations is purely coincidental.

British Library Cataloguing in Publication Data.
A catalogue record for this book is available from the British Library.

Printed and bound by CPI Group (UK) Ltd, Croydon, CR0 4YY
Typeset in 11pt Aldine by Troubador Publishing Ltd, Leicester, UK

Matador is an imprint of Troubador Publishing Ltd

*Dedicated to C, J and M, who occasionally tittered
politely and kept me going.*

*Inspired by the top management guru of all time,
Scott Adams.*

www.dicklannister.com
@dicklannister

Foreword

This marvellous book is written by my friend, colleague and former fag at St Rampton's, Dick Lannister, and contains the dark secrets about how to rise to the top of the work pile without too much effort, secrets that have been kept from the working man or woman for far too long. I am a man but would be perfectly happy to be a woman if the need arose so there is no sexism in this book; sex is no barrier to dancing up the greasy pole to success.

The point is, that being *Le Grand Fromage* is not as hard as you might think. Certainly when I was grand vizier of the Institute of Mediocre Management there was always a worry we'd be caught with our metaphorical trousers down, as it were, if anyone spilt the proverbial beans. Well, now the secret has popped out and contained within these pages is all you need to know to be as successful as I was. Ended up richer than a bent banker, I'll have you know.

I spent forty years in all sorts of businesses, from food processing to nuclear waste and to be honest, same ruddy problems everywhere and the same simple solutions. No one died on my watch, well, not in the nuke job, but they never found Jenkins after he slipped into the vat of meat paste.

So read and learn, dear people. Success, fame and fortune are mere pages away. With an MCA qualification you can lead any business into glorious mediocrity, whilst making a pile in the process and reducing your golf handicap. Well, it certainly worked for me.

Yours insufferably,
Sir Argyll Sutherland Paxton-Beaumont
c/o the West Cheam Home for the Incurably Bewildered

About the Author

Dick Lannister was born in South Burkshire to Mr Lannister and his PA at the time. Quickly showing commercial prowess by selling this story to his prep school magazine, he was rapidly moved to one of England's toughest boarding schools, St Rampton's. Little is known of the 'Dark Years', as he often referred to this period, except that Mr Dark is currently serving time at Her Majesty's convenience.

A straight 'E' student, he went to Oxbreath University to study PPEd (Pottery, Packaging and Eating Disorders) where he emerged three years later with a typing qualification.

His father's school friend, Sir Argyll Sutherland Paxton-Beaumont, gave him his first job as a marketing executive at a food processing company, where his campaign for Road Kill Twizzlers is still talked about today. From there he rose upwards quickly, moving from company to company, gaining promotions whilst leaving issues and challenges in his wake before finally being headhunted to join a top consultancy firm where he mismanaged many contracts, driving stable businesses to the edge of bankruptcy for tax purposes and taking large fees in the process.

Lannister then moved to head up Amalgamated

Industries serving as COO, CEO and finally C3PEO, driving a Strategic Risk Evaluation Management strategy that made the company a small fortune. When his tenure at Amalgamated started they had had a large fortune so it was decided that he should move on to seek other opportunities and challenges.

Unsurprisingly, such incompetence rarely goes unnoticed and he became a director of the Institute of Mediocre Management so his experience could be shared with the glittering leadership talent that frequented its hallowed halls in Bermondsey.

Lannister has written what is now recognised, by his friends, as the leading business management book of the day, *How To Get To The Top – Without Working Too Hard*.

Please note that all proceeds from this book will go straight to his tax-haven bank account so not a penny will be spent on nuclear weapons or battery farming.

Dick is currently married to his fourth wife, Binky, and he understands he has a number of children.

Contents

Introduction

Well done! By starting to read this book you have put your first foot on the ladder to unimaginable success, an unbelievable financial package and the respect and admiration of the great and the good worldwide. Possibly...

This book came about when I was looking out of my office window on the umpteenth floor of a well-known glass office tower in the business district of a world-leading business centre whilst sipping a chilled vodka Martini at the end of a stressless day. Down on the pavement below, the workers were rushing about in the rain, going to appointments or going home to do more work or doing whatever workers do at 17:30. Whilst outside my office, well, actually outside the door of my executive PA's office, my employees, sorry 'colleagues', had their noses to their keyboards, tapping away and making money for me. My smugness at that point knew no bounds as the waft of their envy and fear titillated my nostrils.

Little did they know that when I started my corporate life, I, like them, had quickly realised that I wanted to get to the very top as wealth, power and grovelling respect from underlings seemed more than enough compensation for the occasional late night and all that 'responsibility'. However, I also realised that I was work-challenged so the standard business school route, overtime and working weekends was going to do serious damage to my physical and mental health, as I required lie-ins and copious amounts of alcohol and partying just to survive the daily grind.

And so as I started on the path to success, I watched my co-workers carefully and realised quickly that guile, cunning and general sneakiness were more than adequate substitutes for hard work and long hours. And lack of a moral compass also helped. In fact, as sociopathic traits were a clear behavioural advantage to success, I learnt how to manage, manipulate and scheme my way up the corporate ladder. Always looking for the next step up, I applied for my next job almost as soon as I got a new one, seeking not to join companies who were the best in the field but those organisations that aspired unwittingly to mediocrity.

The clues were generally available by looking at these companies' websites. Organisations that claimed to put the customer first (obviously – duh) but had to say it and who extolled love that knew no bounds for their employees, apart, of course, from low wages and the bi-annual lay-offs or 'reorganisations', and especially companies that had roles with titles of AVPs, VPs, SVPs, ESVPs, and RSVPs, i.e. just jobs for the boys and girls (and therefore me). But the killer clue was finding a Vision Statement on the website, and there's a whole chapter on that in this book, which meant the company would be putty in my manipulative hands.

Back at my existing company, having identified my next role, I would then set about suggesting wild and over-ambitious plans to demonstrate my blue sky, out of the box, strategic thinking whilst in the process upsetting my peers but delighting the board. I would then leave shortly before it all collapsed, leaving others to take the blame and sort it out. Ah, happy days!

Finally the day came when I was first ushered into my very own gigantic wood-panelled office at the top of Amalgamated Industries' vast HQ. I was a CEO and I had made it.

But then my reverie was shattered by a ping announcing an email had arrived. I was mildly irritated that anyone should seek to disturb my tranquility at this ungodly hour. Turning to the computer to open it was the action that changed my life. This email message was the reason I wrote this book and thus created allegedly the world's most successful business course, the MCA, the Master of Corporate Administration.

Everything I learnt and practised successfully is here and success is for the taking. No ulcers, no stress and no troublesome conscience guaranteed. Learn how to smile as you downsize, avoid any association with failure and rise by climbing over the backs of others. Good luck!

And the email message…??! Exactly.

CHAPTER ONE

The MCA Course – An Overview

The **Master of Corporate Administration** or **MCA** is a course for all aspiring and ambitious employees who seek high office, great rewards and love power but want to do as little work as possible in the process. Work really is the curse of modern-day office life. It gets in the way of chatting, thinking, ruminating, postulating and ordering people about. That is, all the fun things about the daily grind and without work, you also get more time for plotting, playing office politics and elbowing your way to the top.

Look at any successful senior manager in your organisation and analyse their actual work output. What is it that they actually do? Round after round of meetings, steering boards, committees and lunches. So ask yourself, have they produced anything that can be touched, tasted, used or smelled? And for such busy bees, where did that golf handicap come from?

The key to success is to delegate almost all tasks and yet retain actual control with the senior management team. This, combined with a carrot-and-stick approach of bonuses and threats of redundancy, ensures the middle managers and worker bees are kept in line. If things actually do go belly up, a business fires some of the lower ranks, reorganises and then carries on as before. This usually corrects the balance sheet.

Executive pay packages and expenses are rarely touched as they underpin the company's success for the future by retaining the right calibre of executive. Senior managers are also not expected to stay for long. They create a five-year business plan but stay only four years. The resulting mess is then picked up by the incoming manager, who reorganises, fires a few more staff for effect and brings in a couple of mates as his management team.

There are a myriad of management courses out there but the main drawback of studying, say for example, an MBA, is that it does involve a lot of hard work and as everyone has one nowadays it doesn't help you stand out anymore. And, of course, you could always buy one online if you really, really want one.

The MCA course covers pretty well all the ground that the plethora of management books, systems and courses that wax and wane in popularity over the years do. Nothing much wrong with any of the ideas that these generate but have you ever wondered how so many books have been written about a subject whose core principles have been understood since Bronze Age bartering? The key one being 'make more money than you spend'.

Many of these books are based on somewhat obvious strategies like: 'Do some actual work rather than have meetings about doing some work', 'Your boss is always right (if you want to keep your job)', or 'Ask people nicely to do things, don't threaten them with a blunt instrument'.

They may also peddle the mantra that you can have what you want, if you want it enough. In reality this is only ever publicly said by the very few who achieved their goals and rarely, if ever, espoused by the 99% who tried to get there and heroically failed.

But the real advantage of an MCA over any other course is that it requires very little work. Simply by reading this book, or if you have a PA, getting them to read it out loud to you, you too can climb the ladders of opportunity aided by the struts of guile, cunning and general sneakiness that this course will teach you.

The MCA course combines the 'important' knowledge imparted by nearly all the world's management books and courses into one volume so at a stroke you save yourself many thousands of pounds, which you can now use to buy something really nice that you've always wanted but didn't think you could afford.

So already you can see that you have achieved success and you are only a few pages into the book. Now persevere to the end of this book and apply the techniques contained within and then you may become richer, get a promotion and finally get to be asked to join the golf club. Then again you might not. But hey, it was ever thus.

MCA Suitability Module

Take this short test to find out if you have got what it takes to join this elite group.

Q1: Your working week should be:
A]   Monday to Friday, nine to five
B]   Eighty-hour weeks and some Sundays
C]   Shift work
D]   It fits around my life

Q2: The CEO calls, do you:
A]   Drop everything and clear your desk for action
B]   Ignore the call as it must be a mistake
C]   Send through a PowerPoint presentation you
     prepared a while ago
D]   Run straight to their office shouting, 'I'm here,
     I'm here…'

Q3: Your team badly screws up so you:
A]   Take full responsibility, fix the damage and then
     offer to resign
B]   Take full responsibility and fix the damage
C]   Promise to fix the damage if you get the time
D]   Blame another department

Q4: A project is:
A]   A series of tasks designed to deliver a defined
     objective.

B] A lot of documents, charts and meetings
C] A series of linked actions defined by a
hypothetical timeline
D] No idea – the workers do that sort of thing

Q5: To communicate with your Mexican office colleagues:

A] Speak to them in Spanish
B] Speak in English but employ a translator
C] Speak in English loudly and wave your arms
D] Use a PowerPoint presentation and suggest they
employ a translator

Answers

Obviously D is the right answer in all the above.

Scores

Five Ds or more:	Well done, you are well on your way to success with little effort and score a bonus point if you went straight to the answers.
Three or four Ds:	That moral compass of yours is pointing in the wrong direction. Adjust and try again.
One or two Ds:	Middle management beckons.
No Ds:	Perhaps an MBA is a better option.

CHAPTER TWO

Mediocrity, Management and Messaging

Mediocrity – An Achievable Goal

There are clear-cut secrets of success for running a business, becoming a leader, increasing your popularity, leading teams, etc. For example: make a profit, treat staff with respect and don't treat customers badly. However, this is too easy and there is no way management could justify large offices, cars, salaries and unlimited expenses if that was all there was to it. It's better to create complex webs of complete piffle to create a fog of misunderstanding but leaves the employee with the worry that it might just be important.

Today's mediocre companies use this business jargon to create a culture which results in woolly thinking at the top permeating into decisions made at the lowest level based on the least effort required. Typically this starts with a 'Vision' statement and ends with a Compromise. Mediocrity's advantage does not require too much hard work.

The five steps to creating a mediocre product

1: Corporate Vision
The CEO and board come up with a Corporate Vision that is usually something blindingly obvious.

'To produce world-class products, supported by excellent customer service that provides really massive stockholder value.'

The question here, of course, is (duh) would you or your competitors do anything else?

This results in a presentation (of course) with two slides, one with picture of happy customers, the second with a graph going in a upward direction which is put together by the CEO's PA. This short presentation is then passed to the VPs or departmental directors for them to develop a corporate strategy to fit the vision.

2: Corporate Strategy

Corporate strategy in mediocre companies is defined as doing something that delivers senior management bonuses and increased stock options in the short term. There is now a bun fight, as everyone wants his or her pet projects and teams involved. Fantastic projects backed by reams of data, bar charts, flow charts and obscure financial terms are proposed on the basis that 'nothing is impossible if you don't actually have to do it'.

A bright young thing on the way up now puts a presentation of sixty-plus slides together. VPs then brief their direct reports on their proposed projects.

3: Middle Management

Middle managers firmly believe they work 24/7 so sit in

glum silence during the presentation. They request additional help and budget to cover the new workload and are turned down. Their next step is to plan exit strategies from the work or how they can pass it on to other colleagues. Finally, with their backs against the wall, they each agree to a project that will take the least time, is easy to do and is hopefully already half complete but hiding under another name. The manager now produces an email informing his staff of the exciting new direction the company is taking and commanding attendance at the next team meeting.

4: The Projects

Workstreams, programmes, project managers and stakeholders are identified. Meetings and workshops are held, action lists compiled, status reports written and conclusions are drawn. Projects that require additional funding, more people or divert staff away from their usual day-to-day tasks are passed back up the chain of command for approval and are then rejected or forgotten about.

5: The Compromise

The Corporate Vision is revisited and changed to fit the compromise and the deliverables are at last agreed. There is a reorganisation, the corporate logo is tweaked and new focus groups are set up. A handful of staff are fired for the benefit of the stockholders, who in return agree to the board's bonus proposals. It is now Q3.

Mediocre Managers v Work-Shy Workers

Underpinning the path to this compromise are the workers. Calling them 'colleagues' or 'associates' may give them delusions of grandeur, but referring to them as 'the little people' is going too far in the opposite direction.

Some of the most successful global organisations are armies, where everyone knows their place and orders are issued and followed and soldiers are often willing to die for their 'company' and its 'bosses'. So this is a good model to follow. Although you should not kill your staff or allow them to be killed as this is expensive and time consuming to resolve and very bad PR.

Another key lesson to remember here is that staff are, in reality, costs and costs impact bonuses. So the fewer the better, and the remainder should work a little harder to cover any shortfall.

It's also important to understand the hierarchy levels within a mediocre company.

Level	Task	Descriptor
Staff ('associate', 'colleague' etc.)	To work	Can be downsized cheaply at will
Supervisor	Make sure staff work	Selects staff to be downsized and can therefore rule by fear
Middle manager	Delegates to supervisors and sits in meetings	Achieve little, take blame, get ulcers. Live in hope of promotion
Senior manager	To have visions	Big picture, big car, big pay cheque

Supervisor and staff positions are a necessary step for MCA graduates to have worked through. You will gain practical knowledge here on how to avoid work, how to cover your tracks and how to manage 'management'. If this is done too effectively, of course, then a 'mediocre' company can become a 'failed' company. Failed companies do not pay salaries or bonuses, so this is not a good path to go down. So it's very important to have a working knowledge of the schemes and strategies that staff will use so that you can prevent the more effective ones that cause the most damage.

It is also abundantly clear that the middle management level is to be avoided at all costs. They are stuck in the middle, neither trusted nor liked by the staff or the senior management. Their task is to implement the impossible. Pass through this level as quickly as possible. No morality is expected here, do what must be done, complete your MCA, as an MCA will help get you to the next level, the senior manager.

Senior Manager

The senior manager has risen high enough in the ranks to ensure he never has to fill in a spreadsheet or follow a 'process' again. That's also why they are often known as 'thought leaders'. They think a lot rather than do a lot.

When you are a senior manager, an ample monthly pay cheque is supplemented by stock options and bonuses. There's a big car in the drive that is looked after and fuelled by the company. There are invitations to speak and conferences in faraway places. First class travel is the norm and public transport is never required as there is always an executive saloon to take you there.

Do note that the size of the company's perceived profits is directly related to a senior manager's financial success. More money makes a senior manager happier so they won't be so grumpy at work, so the staff benefit from this as well.

Senior managers should not sit in an ivory tower all week, and from time to time they should descend to the shop floor and be seen to be part of the team. As part of the team they should lead the employees to greater effort and lower costs.

Now and again there will need to be communication with the staff. In this instance the PR team should take some photos for the in-house magazine of the boss with their sleeves rolled up carrying a box of widgets and then make sure they are plastered around the building. It could be captioned 'Boss Gets Stuck In' or similar.

The next step is to write to the workforce exhorting them to work longer hours for less money. This letter shows that the senior management are on the workers' side as at some, undefined, point in the future they will get their reward. You'll be long gone by then so it will be another manager's headache.

Example Letter One

Dear Associates,

I am writing to let you know that our company, the leading performer in its field, led by a focused, dynamic and first-rate management team, that I personally picked myself, is facing a crisis. I don't want to beat about the bush, so despite the 168-hour weeks worked by your senior management we have realised we cannot do it all ourselves.

So we are asking if you will consider our proposal of working on a little longer at the end the day to ensure our company's survival. Without this our company will be bankrupted and you'll lose your jobs and sadly probably your houses, cars and maybe even your health.

I know that you will join me as we march forward to a glorious future where a shorter working week, bonuses and job security beckon. Your reward for these sacrifices will surely come, but for now you can be proud of being part of our team. The modest pay cut you'll see next week will help us all to survive the slings and arrows of the market.

My kindest regards
Sir Crispin Havealot
CEO
P.S. Xmas party cancelled.

The 'we are in this together' angle is always a useful card to play; it motivates underlings because everyone likes to be in a group. When handing out bad news about wages, try not to be specific. Docking a £100 a week off a worker is a 'modest' pay cut, when compared to a senior manager's salary. The specifics need to be doled out by HR. The workers will think it was their idea to impose draconian measures and the manager can retain that caring exterior. The cancellation of the Xmas party will be expected and funds can be diverted towards a new company car.

If, however, you are of the irritable type then a stronger communication can also be effective. It certainly helps relieve executive stress. Going back to the army analogy, disobedience or not following orders should always be severely punished. Companies can't send them to prison for not delivering 'Project Wally' but they can rattle their cages. This style of letter should do the trick here.

Example Letter Two

Dear Scroungers,

The bad news is that the company is going down the pan thanks to your slouching, lazy and irresponsible ways. My directors and I have had to come in on a Sunday morning in order to try and sort out the mess that you lot created. If you don't pull your collective socks up, I'll be forced to put you back on the dung heap where I found you so you can continue your miserable pointless lives out of my sight.

So starting Monday, your hours go up to eighty per week and your pay is cut by a third. Please feel free to consult with HR, your scabby union or anyone else who has time on their hands to listen to a bunch of whining malcontents. Be assured it will do no good as I'll find out who you are and you will be the first out.

You should also know that I intend to replace most

of you with machines that don't moan, go sick or want paying. I need 'volunteers' to leave this place so don't even think of going to the toilet during work time or having smoking breaks, as you will be the next out on your ear.

So don't say I didn't warn you.

Kindest regards

Sir Crispin Havealot

CEO

P.S. A Merry Christmas to you all!

NB. The P.S. is not mandatory.

Culture Module

Take this short test to find out if you are a sociopath or a wimp.

Q1: Your workers' pay should be:
A] Ahead of the market to attract the right talent
B] Comparable to the market
C] Just below, because your company is the coolest on the block
D] Optional

Q2: To keep morale up in a crisis you should:
A] Organise free drinks and a pep talk at the local pub
B] Hand out free mugs and pens
C] Record a video of you talking incomprehensibly about the market and strategic direction
D] Fire a few people to build up the fear factor

Q3: To cut costs the company has to relocate a long way away so you:
A] Sort a great relocation package because you want everybody to move with you
B] Big it up as a cheaper place to buy or rent property so staff are in reality better off
C] Hand out free mugs and pens with the new postcode on them

D] Move secretly overnight and re-hire at lower wages at the new location

Q4: Company profits have significantly exceeded expectations, what next?

A] Announce free drinks, an Xmas bonus and pay rise for all staff
B] Announce free drinks and an Xmas bonus for all staff
C] Announce free drinks
D] Announce nothing

Q5: How do you want your people to think about your company?

A] Fabulous, fun and friendly
B] Work very hard and play hard occasionally, in my own time
C] Tough, challenging and frightening
D] Prison seems a viable alternative

Answers

For D answers score four points, C three points, etc.
Less than five points: Wimp.
Twenty points: Badass.
Anything in between: Man up.

CHAPTER THREE

Top Ten Meetings

There are many types of meetings: big ones, small ones, some where you get 'actions' and better ones where you can delegate responsibility for your tasks out to other people. These are known as 'productive' meetings.

As an MCA graduate you'll need to know how to create and then manage productive meetings even if your boss initiates them. There are many reasons for calling a meeting such as:

1] Delegation
2] Passing the buck
3] Spreading the blame
4] Telling people your good news
5] Getting other people's ideas so that you can pass them off as your own
6] Fillers for Friday afternoon
7] Team talks
8] Talking with peers
9] Senior management briefing
10] Getting some peace and quiet

1: Delegation meeting

Working hard is really bad for most people; it causes

stress, ulcers, divorce, alcoholism and sleepless nights. This may not impact you today but it could do later on in life so it's better to be safe than sorry, so delegate. Not working hard is not laziness, rather it's doing what you want to do, when you want to do it. Many management books say work 'smart' not 'hard' and this also applies to an MCA graduate, who by definition is pretty smart anyway.

So for example, when your boss hands you his 'to do' list, then you must pass this on in the same spirit. Assemble a meeting, a 'war room' is a good concept and makes the meeting look important. The 'war room' format encourages staff to put all their issues and problems onto sticky notes that are plastered all over the walls of the meeting room. Just add your 'to do' list to the stickies and then ask for volunteers to take 'ownership' of the tasks. Make it clear that everyone will get something, so then it's in everybody's interest to grab the easy stuff first before you delegate the hard stuff to the person who was on the phone, doing their emails or was late.

2: Passing the Buck meeting

This is important as things do go wrong, that's a fact of life but it's still a CLM (Career Limiting Move) if the blame can be placed on your shoulders. Lots more things can go wrong if you have long lunches and don't know what you're doing. And there is the problem, that's precisely what most senior management is about. So there is a real need to have a strategy to ensure that the pointy finger of culpability is not directed at you if the project fails or the budget target isn't met. So organise a 'passing the buck' meeting, which can be approached in two ways.

The first, a 'let's all pull together', 'put the past behind us', 'face the challenge' type affair, where you convince the workers that it was their fault but you are going to help them sort it out because that's the kind of nice person you are. The second is a 'find a scapegoat' meeting, which means you will be firing somebody if this isn't fixed really quickly as there is no way any of this mess is your fault. There's no hard and fast rule on which method to use when, but it's best to vary the style to keep your team on their toes.

Combining the two approaches can have some success. This is where you get your team and another team in the same meeting, heap blame on the other lot and the *schadenfreude* effect on your team should ensure that they'll go through any hoops to sort it out for you. An added benefit is that the two teams will be so absorbed in growling and spitting at each other they'll never think about the root cause, which may have been you.

3: Spreading the Blame meeting

This is a useful technique when your superiors are present but needs to be done subtly as they may spot the strategy. This should never be tried on fellow MCA graduates, of course. A key MCA principle is that any project, task, presentation or proposal should never have been undertaken in the first place unless it was guaranteed success, or a committee undertook it so any blame can be spread widely. But let's take the worst-case scenario in which you were allocated a task, it was clearly identified as your responsibility to carry it out and now it's gone pear-shaped. You'll need to plan this meeting very carefully, as under no circumstances should this become an inquest.

Firstly, you need to write the agenda and the minutes. This extra workload is unfortunately necessary but you can always get back the hours by coming in late the next day. Secondly, the attendees need to be carefully chosen. At least one needs to be a waffler and another the type that gets aggressively defensive. This will help ensure a lack of specific focus during the meeting as well as directing negative energies to these personalities.

Thirdly the aim of the meeting is to 'look forward', realise that this is a 'learning curve' and 'valuable experience' has been gained. Try to focus your attention on the people who rise to this sort of claptrap. Soon they'll be loving you for it and want to be part of the team. Welcome them in, of course, as a spider does to the fly and before they realise it they are part of the solution and by association part of the problem. The *coup de grâce* is to ask them to rise to the challenge and sort it out.

The minutes, which of course you write, will reflect the fact that it wasn't your fault it was everyone else's and secondly, you've taken control, handed out the actions and yet again will lead the project out of disaster into a glorious future.

4: Telling the Good News meeting

Over the course of any year it should be possible to achieve something that can be directly attributable to you. That is much more likely to happen if you have a team whose exploits you can claim credit for. This meeting needs to be carefully advertised as no one else wants to turn up to a meeting to hear how well you've done unless they fall into the 'I am bored, I need a meeting to doze off in' category.

Timing is all-important. An ideal opportunity is when the MD has threatened to prowl around and your colleagues need a bolt-hole. An additional benefit is that prowling MDs tend to drop into meetings unannounced to show that they care. Perfect for you, of course, as you plough through your sixtieth slide of the 'why my division is doing so well' presentation.

Think big, though, when you're creating your good news presentation. 'No one died in my team this year' is a good start. Other safe areas are looking back at known company successes and creating the role you played in them. For example, if your company won a big order and you are in charge of IT you can reasonably claim that your insistence on prioritising the maintenance of the sales force's computers allowed them to focus on their job and win the contract. No one will challenge this because it would seem churlish raining on someone else's parade. This type of good news is teamy and about the only time you associate your success with the efforts of others.

Finding good news that reflects credit on you and you

alone is not hard. For instance, if you are in the habit of coming in early, some MCAs find there is a positive side effect of avoiding the traffic, then you can wax lyrical about your team's time-keeping and focus and how this instilled discipline was crucial in helping your division successfully identify the unexpected challenges thrown up during the last year. Alternatively, if you're habitually late, another way of avoiding the traffic, then you can reasonably suggest that your relaxed but empowering management style help successfully identify the unexpected etc.

5: Getting Other People's Ideas So That You Can Pass Them Off As Your Own meeting

There will always be people who think they can do your job better than you can and, of course, in many instances they are right. However, you don't go round to their house and claim you are a better lover than they are and then proposition their spouse so they should keep away from your turf. You will, in all probability, need to hear what they have to say and if your colleague unexpectedly comes up with a groundbreaking idea that will deliver a better product or service than you could, you should acknowledge this loudly with a, *'Well done, you're absolutely spot on and we are already halfway to implementing this as I thought about this two months ago.'*

Take copious notes, of course, and after the meeting assemble your team and tell them 'your' idea. To be on the safe side, say something about having chatted the whole thing over with the speaker a few weeks ago, for 'his input' just in case he comes back and claims the idea as his own.

Note, of course, that a seasoned MCA graduate will sometimes plant 'great ideas' in meetings where his rivals are present. These ideas will seem feasible and achievable but, of course, they are not. Your colleagues will spend weeks working on these useless and time-consuming projects and will not be bothering you with things they think you should be doing.

6: Fillers for Friday Afternoon meeting

This is self-explanatory. Firstly, you should find a meeting room with a nice view or one that is dimly lit. Secondly, get a junior to present a bunch of slides about his latest project. Thirdly, get lots of people to attend so that you can keep a low profile. Then kick the thing off just after lunch and then doze. That should set you up for the weekend nicely.

7: Team-type meeting

Attendance at some of your team's meetings is sometimes unavoidable but you'll need to ensure that you don't get forced into making decisions, get allocated any actions, or have the finger pointed at you at a later date. Workshops, project meetings and the like are always best avoided and your PA should be briefed to decline any such meeting. Attendance at the first meeting to kick off a project is mandatory though. Do be late and leave early, citing an important meeting with the CEO, or suchlike. First welcome everyone, by name if you can remember them, and then make an inspirational speech about the project being crucial to the future success of the company, or suchlike. Use epithets such as:

1] Top team
2] Accountability and ownership
3] Delivering
4] Where the rubber hits the road
5] Managing expectations
6] Going forward

Single out the project manager for special mention so that he feels he has your backing and so do the others. Remind everyone gently that failure is not an option and if you can drop in something about 'fighting the bean counters off' and 'saving jobs', then so much the better. Fear is a good motivator at the start of a project as it brings a sharp focus to the job in hand for the team. Try not to answer questions during these meetings. Talking continuously and leaving straight after you have finished should prevent this happening. But from time to time some of your more persistent staff will manage to fire off a question. Typical examples of project questions are:

Q: Can you provide us with extra people, resources, money etc?
A: Before I answer that, have you got data regarding the 'number of toasters in Kabul' and 'the percentage of customers with aunts called Edith'?

That is request data that is impossible to get without a whole load of additional work. Your questioner will be diverted and will then be faced with a difficult task to complete or drop the request. 99% will choose the latter.

Q: (The techie-style question) If we increase the rate of data bandwidth into the mainframe surely we'll overload the Cryon database capacity interface, which may well upset our core customers' quark delivery? (Usually followed by smug smile.)

A: Good question. Provide the project manager with a full report with a risk management profile looking forward to 2018 with full financial breakdown of all other alternatives. Monday please and copy me in. (Usually followed by smugger smile.)

Straight after the meeting most project managers will seriously maim the questioner for the additional workload and the lost weekend. The only downside is that you have to leave early and miss the fun.

8: Meetings with your peers

The crucial point for you here is again to control the agenda. This is the highest level of meeting at which there may be actions for you arising out of the items listed. So therefore you need to manage what's on this list, so that means you need to write it. Better still, also volunteer to be chairman and then direct who the actions are allocated to. The agenda should include items that require actions from your peers or that report your team's achievements. If your boss is around it should aim to discuss his pet project, as long as this is progressing well. The agenda certainly should not include anything that is your responsibility or you are associated with that is either not going well, is behind schedule, or may create work for you. If pressed to include such an item, agree to put in Any Other Business. Most meetings overrun and never reach this item anyway. Practise filibustering.

Just in case the occasion arrives when you might get to the AOB, you can always get the meeting to go off topic. For example, tell a weak joke and they'll be queuing up to tell theirs. If it's a more serious meeting, direct a gentle criticism about the performance of a colleague's team and watch the indignant justifications waste the time away.

The last option, of course, is the pre-planned mobile call. Just get someone to call you towards the end of the meeting. When it rings, mutter irritably and say you'll get rid of the call. When you answer the phone, remain silent, look as though you are listening intently and then say, 'Oh, my God!' and then rush out the room. If any one asks you later what the call was about just look tragic and say 'My lips are sealed' and nod your head.

9: Senior Management meetings

This type of meeting is really a get-together for the management to fill up an afternoon. The types of decision that need to be resolved are:

1] Pay rises for the staff – what can we get away with?

2] Pay rises for us – what can we get away with?

3] Car parking – isn't it getting harder to find a place? Should we employ chauffeurs?

4] The company logo – should it be red/blue/green etc?

5] Who's going to have a photo in the company brochure?

Occasionally there are even more serious issues to be resolved. They can be called 'strategic reviews' or 'steering boards' and they deal in the very highest topmost level of decision making The types of decision that need to be resolved are:

a] Keeping stakeholders and analysts happy
This involves formulating a series of requests for data presented in a PowerPoint format that will confuse the stockholders for a while until they can be bought off with higher dividends.

b] Promoting staff
Consensus needs to be reached on who will fit in. This is usually based on the contenders sucking-up ability, their height (short men get cross more easily) and whether they wear the same clothes as the management. Women will be rated on sex appeal by the men, or by their shoes by other women.

c] Saying no to submitted projects
It's important to be seen to have authority and saying no, or at the very least demanding new and better

data, is a good way of reminding the workers just who is in charge. If you want some fun you can always ask one of these junior managers to come up and present to you all.

This works even better if you've already postponed the presentation at least once beforehand. Let the guy set up the projector and their laptop whilst you all stare at him in silence. By the time he kicks off he should be a nervous wreck. At the end; be generous, thank him politely, ask him for more data so that you can come to a more informed decision and then as he leaves and closes the door, all burst out laughing. He'll never know whether it was his presentation or something else that caused the mirth.

10: Getting Some Peace and Quiet meeting

This type of meeting is needed when the previous night, you agreed to go for one quick drink after work but that turned into two and then it was your round and the rest is a blur. And you woke up still wearing your suit. Having exhausted all other options: throwing a sicky (did that last time), bereavement (run out of aged aunts), or working from home (last night's brilliant idea of cleaning the keyboard with a beer put paid to that), you had to reluctantly head for the office powered by painkillers and black coffee.

You may well survive till after lunch but after what you did to yourself last evening, even the God of Thunder would have a Thor★ head in the afternoon. So

★ This kind of cheap gag does not occur again.

book a meeting room with no windows and go there with a cup of paperclips. Close the door and scatter them on the floor by the door. Go to sleep with your feet pressed against the door. If you should be disturbed you can open the door on your knees and start to pick up paperclips. NB. Check the door opens inward as this doesn't work if it's the other way round.

Meetings Module

Take this short test to find out if you are a crowing rooster or a lame duck chair.

Q1: Meetings should:
A]   Be pre-planned with agendas and objectives
B]   Have a purpose
C]   Be a chance to show off to peers
D]   Be an opportunity to spend time away from the PC

Q2: Minutes of a meeting are:
A]   A true record of what happened in the meeting
B]   A true record of the bits that happened that the writer remembered
C]   A copy of the agenda with some unintelligible notes
D]   A reflection of the outcome that the writer wanted

Q3: A team meeting is:
A]   An opportunity to get together to swap information and progress on projects
B]   An opportunity to suck up to the boss
C]   Time to catch up with some emails
D]   An opportunity to delegate your workload

Q4: A vendor meeting is:

A] A two-way discussion trying to get the best deal for both parties

B] A one-way discussion trying to fleece the vendor

C] A one-way tirade of threats trying to ruin the vendor

D] An opportunity to see if there are any good jobs going with the vendor's company

Q5: A board meeting is:

A] A gathering of top management looking to increase company profits and success

B] A gathering of top management looking to remove costs and employees

C] A gathering of top management looking to get one over on their rivals on the board

D] A gathering of top management looking to increase remuneration, share options and bonuses

This was a trick test, because if you had read the chapter and taken notes you would have scored full marks. If you did, you can take Friday afternoon off. If you didn't, then you will need to volunteer to run the next company charity day.

CHAPTER FOUR

Finance – Money, Money, Money

The vast majority of the world's population understands the basic rules of finance. Go to the poorest country, into its deepest jungle and even in the smallest hut in the remotest village, the key principle of company economics is clearly understood. And the simple model that actually underpins the ecosystems of the world's largest conglomerates?

If you spend (buy, barter, exchange) more than you receive, then you're in trouble.

Sadly there are a few key areas in the world where this rule is often not applied or sometimes not even understood. This place is the boardroom. If anyone could be bothered to research the lifestyle of most board members it would probably reveal that their partner does the home finances or they'd all be living in abject poverty.

So why does company finance appear so complicated? Because it's a black art, not a science. No company could ever expand fast enough to deliver high rewards for the typical 'I want it all and I want it now' attitude of today's stockholders and owners unless the books could be massaged. This also applies to when a company is heading down a slippery slope to oblivion; time is needed for the executives to bail out with reputations and bonuses intact. And most of this massaging is perfectly legal, so investors beware.

Finance Basics

The basic accounting principle is defined by the bean counters as:

$$Assets = Liabilities + Owner's\ Equity$$

What are Assets?

Assets are what is in the bank, what you're owed, the stuff in the warehouse, the products required to make the things in the warehouse and the warehouse itself. The trouble is, that in the real world this well-meaning concept fails to deliver accurate financial accounts. In reality, the majority of companies have no idea what stock they own. This is often because when they upgraded the IT system to manage the stock control they downsized the warehouseman to pay for it. The problem here was that he was the only one who knew what was what, and where it was.

The products in the warehouse are now either well past their use-by date or not the right parts for the mark-two version that was recently launched. This last issue was caused after the last reorganisation downsized the logistics department. Then the procurement director's bonus was made payable based on the size of cost reductions rather than the cost-effective purchasing of parts and spares. And then finally the warehouse was mortgaged a while back by a VP who turned that year's results into the best ever by a complicated corporate refinancing and accounting manoeuvre where the remortgage bit was hidden on page 47 of the supporting spreadsheet and noted on slide 104 as a sub-note explaining the move. The VP received an excellent bonus that year before moving on to a competitor where he acquired 50% of his previous company's customers based on speed of delivery of the new company's goods.

What are Liabilities?

Liabilities are what you owe and probably also define most of your senior management team. For the non-financially minded, they are the sum of the numbers in the filing cabinets and the in-trays of 'accounts payable'. The accounts payable team is usually in an office tucked away at the end of the building where no one ever goes. No one is ever sure how many people work there because to enter that room would be to subject yourself to an hour of bought-ledger balancing or the deficiencies of the IT system. It's the black hole of finance as much more goes in than ever comes out. Getting a cheque out of this department is a daunting task and must be approached with patience, humility and an unflappable personality. Never ever shout down the phone at an accounts payable employee, it will not work and your chances of getting cooperation in the future will be virtually nil.

To get a total of your firm's liabilities, therefore, there's no point in asking for this year's accounts. If asked nicely they will grudgingly hand over a set around two years old and usually this is close enough to use for this financial year.

What is Owner's Equity?

If you take all your assets and take away the liabilities that is the owner's equity. Or in other words, the value of what the stockholders own. Basically not much or it's a negative sum so it's not really worth bothering about. There are times when it's necessary to ensure that the owner's equity is a significant sum. For instance when cashing in share options.

The easiest way to do this is to inflate the asset value and reduce the liabilities. It's paper exercise and not something based in any reality and this is called refinancing. It's important to remember that as an MCA graduate you have to have an ability to keep a company going for a while even if it doesn't benefit you right away. This is not being altruistic, it's simply a key necessity that allows you to buy time to ensure that when you make your move it's at the right moment for you.

MCA Accounting Principles (MCAAP)

So if the accounting rules defined by the standard financial textbooks are only valid in the classroom, how do you run the money side of a mediocre company in the real world? You will need to use the MCAAP economic model.

Principle One: Revenue should be greater than costs

Here revenue is real money, not 'things', promises, future earnings or anything else like that. You only use that type of money to fool analysts or people who may want to buy you out.

Costs are everything that you have to pay for now and in the future related to that revenue plus estimated variables and 'intangibles'. Note that intangibles are the key metric here.

Principle Two: Profit is a good thing

This is the sum of money left after you've paid all your bills. And by bills, it's *all* the bills. That is: interest, amortisation, Capex, Opex and the bits you borrowed to tide you over till the end of the month. Many financial courses teach managers how to hide costs and increase revenues by moving money around, or how a company can sell things back to itself. Enron and the banking crisis were classic examples of this *modus operandi* so there are a number of significant risks doing this. An MCA graduate would realise that this is hard work and sometimes illegal and, of course, an MCA graduate is far too clever to end up in jail. So financial figures need only be massaged until the annual bonuses are paid.

Principle Three: Intangibles dictate financial momentum

Intangibles are defined as 'difficult for the mind to grasp'. These are part of the costs equation and probably the key reason why companies fail. Most CFOs cannot get their head around this type of nebulous idea. An intangible is an effect that can derail a company, like poor staff morale, a bungled reorganisation, or a dramatic and sudden impact, like a fire.

The complex and detailed spreadsheets that tend to support business cases are unable to quantify intangibles. Line after line of revenues, costs, Capex, Opex and depreciation, but nothing about broken photocopiers, the hiring of an incompetent middle manager, or moving the office to Milton Keynes. A simple photocopier failure is often the incarnation of the Chaos Theory's 'Beat of a Butterfly Wing' impact. It starts a process of destruction that can topple global conglomerates.

There are many external intangibles, like an economic slowdown, war, or bad weather and again these never appear on spreadsheets. As an MCA graduate you need to slice off a suitable percentage of the optimistic forecast of success that some young pup has put in front of you and then submit that number as your bonus target.

Remember also, as your grandmother said, 'It's important to put something away for a rainy day'. Call it investment, savings or anything else you want to but it should be in a nice secure place that pays interest. And count it as a cost. If it's a significant amount it will pay good interest. This should not be spent or reinvested but should be put by to deal with intangibles. Just before year-end, it can be magically produced under the guise of additional sales and suddenly the company has 'exceeded expectations'. This is a good thing. So armed with this knowledge, now is the time to build a business plan which includes intangibles.

Intangibles Underpin Business Plans

Let's look at these intangibles in more detail. The business plan drives the financial numbers for projects and determines whether, at some point in the not-too-distant future, more money will come in than was actually spent.

Usual accounting principles would see a column of revenues expected, or 'money in', and a column of the costs associated with these expected revenues, or 'money out'. The difference would be the company profit. However, even this simple model cannot tell the whole truth. Driving this model are intangibles.

1: Staff morale
If it's high, then the project will succeed as your staff will find a way to work around the things the VP forgot to include in the requirements. If it's low, then the project team will either let the project die or will make excessive demands for additional people, equipment and time. At best, the project will be completed but late and at huge additional cost.

2: The board gets bored
Most senior management have a very short attention span; for some it's hours, for most it's about a week. By

then they've moved on to the next exciting thing. This change of mind is often described as being 'ahead of the game', 'visionary' or 'thought leadership'.

The fall-out is that programmes and projects wither on the vine as executive support fades away and are then cancelled. No one ever then removes the revenue benefit from the budget forecast but the costs disappear and the shareholders think the CEO is wonderful for 'driving up the margin'.

3: Corporate finance

Skulking behind the board is the corporate finance team. They can add up in their heads a string of numbers that mere mortals struggle with using a calculator. They will often demonstrate this at meetings with a smug smile. Sadly, they almost always lack any emotional intelligence and so intangibles are never factored in. It's impossible to argue with them, though, as they can only work with data or 'metrics'. They also add in their 'assumptions' which move the final numbers up or down depending on whether they think the project is a good idea or not.

4: Incompetent managers

Incompetent managers can massage a presentation or status report in their sleep and will provide years of convincing evidence on how well their departments are doing before the whole thing comes crashing down. Often the senior manager moves on up or out of the company and the successor has no idea what he's sitting on top of and so the cycle starts again.

5: The competition

There is a simple financial equation to quantify the impact of the competition on your business plan:

$$nC = P/n$$

where 'C' is the competition's competence, 'P' is your profit and 'n' is the 'we're better than you' number. For example: If the competition is twice as successful as you, then your hoped-for profit will be halved.

6: The marketing and sales departments

These marketing guys can be really dangerous, as a good idea badly sold will fail. Marketing people believe they are cleverer, brighter and more important than sales. So it's not for them to create a simple and clear message. They develop compelling customer propositions, which confuse the hell out of the man on the road tasked to sell this to the customer. Inevitably, the message is delivered wrongly and sales plummet amidst a welter of finger wagging and blame.

Plummeting sales is not good for the sales department as they have incentives based on what is actually sold, i.e. the more you sell the more you make. A salesman will therefore do whatever it takes to close a deal, including wildly exaggerating the product's capabilities and also dropping the discounted sale price to a fraction of its cost to make.

7: Focus groups and research

Many new product ideas are based on focus groups and customer research. In reality, this often means a couple of apocryphal stories and writing up what the research director's wife and kids thought. This rarely reflects the market and so the product is often developed on foundations of sand.

8: Mistakes

It comes as a surprise to many managers that they make mistakes and their teams make mistakes. Because of this, mistakes are nearly always covered up. But the consequences ripple through and can often significantly impact the end result.

Intangibles summary

So it should now be clear that an amount of money should be set to one side to cover any of the above scenarios that may affect your company's projected profitability. This can be invested in a high-interest savings account or kept in a large brown envelope in the company safe. Whatever happens, do not spend it.

Financial Terms

The MCA graduate also needs to make themselves acquainted with a rudimentary knowledge of financial terms. This gives a semblance of financial acumen and shows you are playing the game properly.

1. EBITDA

The word profit went out of fashion years ago when it

was realised that such a simple concept could be understood by most sentient beings. This knowledge therefore did not justify the high salaries that accountants and finance managers expected, so they invented another term. It's called EBITDA and pronounced Ee-beet-t'daah. More importantly is the way you pronounce it so you sound as though you know what you're talking about. It stands for 'Earnings before Interest, Taxation, Depreciation and Amortisation'. There's no need to know the detail. It's merely a way that you can express a profit without there really being one by hiding a bunch of costs somewhere else on the balance sheet.

Revenues, costs and other financial measures are called 'metrics' and not 'totting up the cash', 'collecting wonga', or 'splashing the dosh', unless you work on a trading desk in a financial centre. Knowing the actual value of these metrics is a key to success for a typical VP. For an MCA graduate it's about knowing your boss's favourite ones. These are the metrics he'll have memorised in order to drop into a conversation to show he's on the ball.

2. Forecasts

There are different types of budgets or forecasts. Top-down forecasts are the budgets imposed on the lower orders by senior management. They reflect what the shareholders want to hear and are achievable only by cutting costs, redundancies, freezing pay and postponing anything that costs money to do. The workforce doesn't like this type of budget imposition so it needs to be sold by the management. For example, fire the protestors' ringleaders as this usually brings everyone back in line.

Bottom-up forecasts are created by the company's middle managers and reflect their hopes and aspirations, the hopes being less work and the aspirations being higher pay. In this type of forecast there will be a higher headcount, a new departmental structure for them to lead and upgrades to any technical or operational equipment.

Both these budgets are fairytales. For an MCA the original budget numbers are not important, as they are out of date as soon as they have been published due to non-forecasted intangibles. Just provide what is required to make you look great and remember there's a whole year ahead to create something that will look like a profit.

3. The re-forecast

A key tool to delivering this profit is the re-forecast. Many companies have one every quarter but you could have twelve a year if you wanted. In fact, the more the merrier as many a financial 'dead body' can be hidden in here. The key principle of a re-forecast is to balance the likely actual revenues and costs with the new forecast. Better to make them worse, so that at the end of the next re-forecast period you can show you 'exceeded budget expectations'.

Instead of losing £1 million you only lost £750K, which shows a positive trend, and a positive cash flow is certain in the next fiscal year. If a smart alec asks why the original budget predicted a profit, just say 'That's not forward looking so get with the team and stop being negative'.

4. Audits

Once a year a special breed of accountants invades the company and runs through the financial numbers. They have no friends, no sense of humour and are not to be bribed. Even mugs with slogans and company tee shirts don't work with these people. This is the time when an MCA graduate should be on holiday.

Finance Module

Are you a 'money metrics maestro' or a 'Nobby no-mates number-cruncher'?

Q1: A balance sheet:
A] Is an auditable record of the company's finances
B] Is a record of the company's finances best kept away from a competent auditor
C] Is a collection of financial metrics that makes quantum theory look easy
D] Reflects what the CEO said he would achieve at the beginning of the financial year

Q2: A departmental budget:
A] Is the amount of money required to deliver the agreed objectives
B] Is 50% over the amount required to allow for the inevitable trimming during the budget process
C] Is a wild guess based on what happened last year
D] Could win first prize in a children's fiction writing competition

Q3: A business case:
A] Demonstrates if there is a good cost-versus-benefit case for the planned work
B] Conveniently supports a good cost-versus-benefit case for the planned work

C] Uses any assumptions, forecasts and Googled metrics that prove the proposer's plans

D] Should be worked to support any objectives of the vision statement

Q4: Profit is:

A] A way of showing a company is making money for the benefit of its workforce and stockholders

B] The reason companies go into business in the first place

C] An opportunity to siphon off a bit of cash to pay for executive treats

D] Something that needs to be spent quickly before the taxman gets sight of it

Q5: An accountant is:

A] A clever person who understands how financial metrics and markets work

B] A slightly dull person who understands how financial metrics and markets work

C] A person who says 'no' to even the most reasonable request for funding

D] The person with the power to support your bonus payment request

Answers

For correct quartile responses, excluding off-shore point taxation deductions count as a share equity score. Non-compliant, but partially sustainable question responses should be taxed at the higher rate but still qualify for deductible points. Any other answers please refer to the Accountancy Almanac 1981.

Write your score here: ....

CHAPTER FIVE

Perfect Projects

An MCA graduate's projects rarely fail and if they do, these failures are never traceable back. They don't usually fail because the required outcome is either already achieved or the delivery date is so far in the future that the project will either be cancelled due to cost cutting or is no longer aligned to the corporate strategy.

Projects That are Worth Doing

1. Copying your competitor

Find a product that your competitors are selling and then do the same. Copying is the sincerest form of flattery, plus as they are likely to be better than you, the fact they are doing it means it has got to be a good idea.

2. From any management book

Just filter the ideas from a bestseller like *Thirteen Habits of Smug Know-alls* to fit your company profile, plus if it goes pear-shaped, then you can always say 'Conglomerate Plc did this successfully in 1995 and it was someone else's fault that it didn't work here'.

3. The standard 'can't fail to impress' projects list

a] Cost reduction by downsizing the workforce.

b] Departmental reorganisation.

c] Firing the existing provider of an outsourced function and hiring another similar company.

The Project Team

The Project Manager

Project managers organise stuff, like meetings, actions and risk registers. Be nice to the PM because you don't want any actions assigned to you. The project manager is ideally a contractor so can be blamed and then fired if things are not going well.

The Programme Manager

They provide progress and status reports, plus presentations. Can also be wheeled in front of management to explain what is happening, saving you the time finding out. Also need to be kept on-side, as the presentations they create will be used by you to justify your job.

The Deputy

They take notes and tell your peers and other stakeholders what to do and then hound them, whilst you take on the onerous task of handing out the plaudits and any good news.

The Expert

The only person on the project team that knows what they are doing and also has the details. They are usually passionate and incomprehensible but vital or you'll deliver a chocolate kettle – lovely but useless.

The Stakeholders

Usually a couple of appropriate middle managers. Their teams are supporting the project or delivering parts of it. They don't want to be there as this is extra work for no benefit to them. Don't make eye contact or you'll get excuses.

The PA

Fierce ones round everyone up by reorganising their diaries for you. Friendly ones bring you buns and can get you out of meetings when you need to exit fast.

Project Tasks and Actions

These are perfect storms of overlaps and infighting. This is good as you can use the teams' antagonism towards each other to ensure they don't bother you with any trivia or work and by showing favouritism to individuals to ensure that they suck up to you and do your bidding rather than the team's.

Briefing the team:

In a nutshell, you need to communicate that it's a key

deliverable for the board, you're only interested in the big picture so you don't want problems, only solutions, and as a motivator add that if it doesn't come together on time and on budget they are all fired, sorry, downsized.

Updates
Demand monthly updates, or weekly if you think you can get away with it, as a full-blown, chart-ridden, metric-heavy presentation. These should be twenty or thirty slides and need a one-page executive summary of the important bits, as you won't have time to read the rest.

Report back to the board
This should be monthly and saying how well it's going. Don't take anything but the summary to the meeting or some clever clogs is going to start questioning the data. If asked to provide more detail, simply say you will take an action to get back to them on that and then castigate your team for not including the answer in the summary. Also remember to never get back to a questioner with an answer they don't want. Better not to get back to them at all, if possible, as it will only encourage further questions.

Actions
These are tasks that need to be completed before the next project meeting. Think bubonic plague here. Keep away from actions and anyone who might give you one. To stretch this tenuous metaphor further, if you are a carrier, then feel free to infect others.

Steering boards

An unfortunate fact of life is that things don't always go to plan and because you are an MCA you don't have a Plan B anyway. So if a project you are leading is going pear-shaped, start looking for scapegoats. Your project team members are the first obvious choice and you may need to throw one or two to the wolves during the project anyway. To paraphrase a French admiral commenting on the execution of an English admiral: 'It's to encourage the others.'

However, this is small fry and the action is expected. The crucial requirement is to involve your peers, so set up a 'steering board' for the project. This needs to include the senior management of any department involved or affected by your project. At this level they won't be 'detail' people so you can get away with telling them very little. Keep it simple and talk about 'joined-up approaches', 'key issues being addressed' and 'corporate governance'. Your steering board will lap this up and by the mere fact that they turned up can now be allocated partial blame in any cock-up.

Project end

There are two types of project endings. The first finishes on time, on budget and achieves its objectives. This type doesn't concern us here, as it is a very rare occurrence and you just have to claim the plaudits. In reality, most projects fizzle out when either it's clear it won't work, or when the collateral damage to the rest of the organisation becomes so great that your colleagues get nervous and jump overboard, i.e. they stop turning up to meetings.

Both are positive results. There's no blame attached and you are remembered for the positive reports that indicated clearly you were on top of the task the whole time it was running. You can also afford to look slightly disappointed that the project was ended and will get some sympathy from the senior management for its cancellation. Always, of course, put a brave face on it and say how you can also see the 'big picture' that they can and fully understand and support their wise decision to can it.

Project methods

To complete a project there are formal processes that determine how the thing will be run, and today there are two main methodologies that most project managers use. They are the 'Waterfall' or 'Agile' methods.

Basically, Waterfall is the older-style project management way of doing things. A business analyst defines the project requirements in great detail, the product manager puts together a timeline and budget and the project manager then makes sure everyone does what they are supposed to do.

This works well if the instigators of the project and the various stakeholders had, a) bothered to read the original documentation, and b) turned up to the workshops when this was discussed.

Usually the first reaction the project team get is when the prototype is demonstrated and then there's a plethora of comments like, 'Why doesn't it do this?', 'Why don't you add this?', or 'I'm not paying for that, it's not what I want'. Then comes the agony of implementing change control to resolve the issues, which then screws up the timeline and the budget. Eventually something is delivered which is a compromise, delivered late and is far more expensive than at first thought.

The solution to this was Agile. This allows an agreed idea to start its development from a concept and 'use cases' (i.e. how it works in real life) rather than formal documentation. Each cycle of development is called a 'sprint' and lasts two weeks. Meetings to discuss the output and agree the success of each cycle are known as 'scrums' and the person who runs these is the 'scrum master'. For some strange reason, people are expected to stand during scrum meetings.

A quick digression here, a 'scrum' is a rugby term for eight players that bind together, crouching and not standing, when someone has broken a 'law of the game'. There is no 'master' and these players, also known as 'forwards' and being built for pushing and the occasional violent attack on the opposing team, are not habitually 'sprinters'. But put this to one side for now.

After each cycle, changes can be made to the previous work and the new tasks for the next cycle are agreed. In reality, although the initial plan was to deliver an automobile, the end result will be a unicycle. However, everybody is happy with this as they agreed to the changes en route.

Projects Module

Take this short test to find out if you are a 'master' or 'unfit for purpose'.

Q1: A project delivers:
A]   The original project requirements
B]   A lot of paperwork and workshops
C]   Something quite similar to the things you have already, but not quite as good
D]   What the boss mentioned in passing at a team meeting

Q2: Project requirements are:
A]   A list of things that the thing should do
B]   A list of things that the thing should do but will cost too much to deliver
C]   A list of things that the thing should do, which changes daily
D]   A list of things the thing does, that is discovered after the thing is launched

Q3: A project manager's key role is to:
A]   Drive the project forward, making sure it's on time and on budget
B]   Draw up a timeline with swim lanes★

★ Don't ask, you really don't need to know, life is far too short…

C] Allocate actions to everyone and moan until they are completed

D] Buy cakes and buns so the team gets a sugar rush and agrees to do the actions

Q4: Is a Kanban:

A] A visible workflow from which tasks are allocated by a scrum master

B] One level higher than a black belt in origami

C] When the scrum master says no fizzy drinks are allowed in the meeting

D] To be ignored, as actions are for the team, not you

Q5: Projects usually fail because of:

A] Incompetence

B] Apathy

C] Budget reallocated

D] All of the above

Answers

The right answers will be made available when this book project is finished.

More than three stickies, you get one highlighter.

More than five stickies, you get three highlighters.

More than ten stickies you get a complete set of highlighters and a board rubber.

CHAPTER SIX

Marketing – Fibbing Your Way to Success

Marketing is another Dark Art. People who can, do, people who can't, market.

This is slightly unfair as the vast majority of us succumb to the market flannel most days of the week. Almost everything we buy, from branded clothes, to faddy food or personal transportation, has been coated with the slime of want, rather than the sheen of need. Harnessing this flaw in the human condition is the aim of every marketer. Apart from extremist Puritans and the Amish, everyone else on the planet is susceptible to these messages.

Customer Value Proposition

This is the key idea of marketing. Any marketing book will talk about the CVP, which is then analysed to death. In essence, a CVP requires a company to sell the right product at a reasonable price to a customer who might actually want it. The Chartered Institute of Marketing puts it more wordily:

> *'Getting the right goods, to the right people, in the right place, at the right time, at the right price, with the right level of communication, profitably.'*

Considering this organisation is full of the type of people who should be able to deliver snappy, memorable and easy-to-remember sound bites, this statement seems a little cumbersome. And there were too many 'rights', right?

Marketing vs Selling

To an MCA graduate, marketing is the art of selling something at a significant profit to someone who doesn't really want it. This is not a difficult thing to achieve. It requires a little confidence, a flexible approach to morality and access to a large expense account.

Selling is, we are told, not the same as marketing. Of course, it isn't. Selling means travelling around the country with an attaché case full of brochures. Salesmen live in crumbling motels near major road junctions and seek only in life, a larger car with more accessories than the salesman parked next to them. Marketers rarely leave the head office in the big city unless it's for a foreign photo shoot. There are lunches, corporate entertainment events and strategy meetings to attend. The only link with the sales force is the brochure.

How Sales and Marketing works

Salesman: Good morning. I have wonderful time-saving device that will save you hours of dull housework, allowing you to join a health club, visit exotic faraway places and meet the man of your dreams.

Customer: It's a brush.

Salesman: It's a micro-particle remover.

Customer: I've got one.

Salesman: I can see you're no fool, so I'm going to reduce the price and pay the difference out of my wages, from £100 to £1.49.

Customer: Done!

And, of course, the customer is, but the salesman used the classic techniques of creating aspirations, talking the product up and then offering a 'bargain'. Who can resist that?

The marketer believes *they* were, in reality, responsible for the sale, as they produced the brochure and, of course, will claim all of the credit. The brochure will have featured sex, as it's very hard to sell dull things unless you drape something more interesting around it. Ideally the brush would be held by a tanned, steely-eyed toy-boy holding it just so, in order to hide any embarrassment or start legal proceedings. A cover line like 'It's Long and Bristly' will ensure the message gets home.

The message, of course, is the key; in the crowded

consumer marketplace your company's brush has to stand out. If it doesn't, you don't get a pay rise so don't get all moral when manipulating the message.

Customer Focused

Being customer focused is the most common phrase used in the mission statements of big corporations. Unsurprisingly, it is usually the case that customer focus is way down the list of the business's priorities for their staff, whose attention is focused on their careers, avoiding work and putting one over on their colleagues. To be fair, this is not surprising as dealing with customers is not a pleasant experience. Cast your mind back to when you last called in to Global Widgets. Was it to praise them for all their hard work? Thank them for providing you with a widget that really was as life-changing as their brochure suggested? Or was it to report that the bloody thing turned up three weeks late with a bit missing?

The problem is that all customers have been encouraged to be 'empowered' and not to take no for an answer, even if they are probably wrong. We're told to tweet the top man, write letters to our MPs, demand compensation; in effect, cause problems.

Companies that actually care about this sort of thing spend large amounts of time placating the obnoxious to the detriment of spending time with the cooperative. The obnoxious rarely buy anything again and are usually compensated significantly so the economics for this customer-focused strategy don't look good.

Of course, a company could get their product right in the first place but as it's usually been created based on information gleaned via customer focus groups and apocryphal research, it's unlikely to be successful. Asking a bunch of inebriated, opinionated people who really need to get out more, to define your product strategy is flawed reasoning. And these are the self same people who will crucify you a year later when you launch the merchandise.

The Four Ps

The four Ps are the cornerstone of marketing strategy.

Definition	In Practice
Product – What it is	You'll need a new one next year
Price – What it costs	Very cheap but spares cost a fortune
Place – Where can you get it	Ask the sales department
Promotion – Telling everyone about it	Still discussing the logo

Product

The customer always wants a lot of features such as a mobile telephone which will teleport them anywhere in the world, when in reality you've got a low-spec phone that you can carry to anywhere in the world but cuts out if you walk more than twenty metres away from a mast, even shorter if someone walks in front of it.

To the marketing department, the aspirations are not really all that different, at least you are both talking the same language. Officially this difference in product specification is called 'gap analysis'. Generally speaking this is more like 'chasm analysis' as customers want lots of things for nothing. Marketing, of course, is all about convincing them they have achieved this goal.

Marketing solve this issue by running a competition for your phone buyers where the first prize is to travel somewhere abroad. You can use the word 'teleport' in the marketing materials. A line or two in the small print will overcome any legal implications.

Price

Prospective customers will want the teleporting telephone for the price of a Greggs doughnut whilst your business plan confidently projected they would willingly sell close relatives into slavery and hand over the house in order to get their hands on one. This is known as price elasticity.

Place

Now you have your product, where are you going to sell it? Teleporting phones are not usually available in car boot sales, unless, of course, they've been ripped off. So some legwork is required to understand where you're going to sell this and how you're going to get it there.

Your marketing executive should provide you with a list of everywhere and anywhere. The next step is to hive off the international bits for yourself and get the PA to organise the trip. As you're doing the smooching, you're responsible for the dinner invitations, which means you get to choose the restaurants. Life just got better.

The other members of the team get the local and provincial visits. A good way to keep costs down, as you don't want them eating into the department's expense budget, is to suggest they rent a camper van and use the many facilities available at motorway service stations. A win-win here is to get them to talk to sales, who are likely to be in the car park at the same time.

Promotion

Now you need to tell everybody about your wonderful product. Think TV at first because it's glamorous and you get to meet stars. Insist that your advertising agency book an 'A-list' celebrity to present the commercial and then insist they organise lunch with them. The ability to successfully name-drop is a key MCA requirement. After lunch, a visit to the TV studios and some good old boot licking by the agency, claim your budget has been taken away and you'll need to settle for a junk mail shot.

Junk mail is singularly responsible for the deforestation of huge swathes of rainforest but the positive aspect is that it's easy to do, cheap and doesn't require a lot of hard work. The other advantage is that hardly anyone reads junk mail so you won't get a rush of orders and phone calls, which can be intensely annoying on a Monday or a Friday. And absolutely no one reads the small print. Even if they wanted to, they couldn't, as obviously you instruct the printer to use a micro font and then print the prose in pink on a red background. This means that you can say 'free' or '£500 off' over the top of a pouting girl or man, depending on the market, and then qualify everything in the small print. Using the phrase 'none of the above is true' is a good catch-all. This also means you don't even have to get the facts right, which is always a real nuisance as it's really time consuming.

Market research

Sometimes at senior management meetings a colleague will ask why you think the company should produce your product or sell your service.

This is to be expected, as wrong-footing peers is a key method of putting rivals down and making themselves look good. As an MCA graduate, however, you need to be able to parry such an attack and then counter it. Research allows you to appear objective about your product. 'It's what the customer wants,' you say and produce a large presentation with lots of charts. The longer the presentation, of course, the more believable it is. There's no way they'll let you get to the end of a fifty-pack of customer research slides anyway as they'll be struck down by terminal boredom by slide five at the latest. They'll agree to anything rather than go through another two hours' worth of data.

It's important to also remember that 'good' research

is asking the right question to ensure the answers meet your needs or your boss's needs, especially if he has already sold the idea to the board.

Research questions

To get the right answer for the 'teleporting' phone to be sold at an exorbitant price, you need to ask the right questions to get the right answers. For example:

1] Do you think phones are useful?
2] Is free travel a good idea?
3] Would you ever consider selling your house?
4] In an emergency, would you leave a dependent with someone else for a few days?

With some minor usage of assumptive data application, it's clear that customers will want your new phones and will also sell their relatives and houses to get hold of one, so long a you offer a prize of a holiday.

Research can also be used to find out how well a company is doing. For example, they could ask, 'How good is our service?' This is a highly dangerous avenue to go down but it's used as an illustrative example. Usually the research company would ask the respondent to tick a box from a choice of five marked:

Hopeless, Bad, Average, Good and Excellent.

This is not a good list of differentiators for a question like this. A better selection of descriptors would be:

Not Bad At All, Pretty Good, Above Average, Excellent, Superhuman.

That way you're going to get a positive result whatever the whinging low lifes try and pin on your company.

Focus groups

Another type of research is the focus group. A company rounds up a representative sample of its customers and then, using a neutral moderator, asks them a set of questions relating to their products or services. In reality, as these events are usually staged on a wet Tuesday night in a room in a business park, getting a representative group together is near impossible. This is no bad thing as you're rarely after facts; remember you need opinions that match your own, as these are much better for your career than hard truths.

Your core focus-group member is a veteran of product research, ranging from jam tasting to soft furnishing colours; they have smelt things, touched things and worked things. They've been offered tea, coffee, wine, beer, sandwiches and canapés. They've been questioned, flattered, smiled and frowned at. In short, they are battle-seasoned veterans. Crucially, they have the experience to realise that their opinions don't actually matter unless they coincide with those of the company that booked them in the first place. They will have an opinion about your firm and its products but this will be based on the quality of the catering. It is, therefore, extremely important to properly research who is actually going to turn up. Are they beer or wine drinkers? Sandwiches or canapés? Afternoon or evening session? Careful preparation of these key details will deliver a group that will be putty in your hands.

The product life cycle

This is another phrase beloved by marketers which describes the start of product development, or when you invent or create something, i.e. when it's born, to the time when your competitor has managed to copy your idea and produce a version, which is twice as good at half the price. Then it's killed.

The marketing plan

The marketing role revolves around the marketing plan. From account executive to marketing director, this document is their purpose and focus. The plan outlines all the things that will be done to promote and sell their company's products and how effective these activities will be. This is obviously a very dangerous document as it has targets, or KPIs to use the vernacular (Key Performance Indicators). Targets mean measurements and that means working hard to achieve them and possibly, or probably, missing them.

So a true MCA marketing plan is firstly complicated so it's not understandable by anyone outside the team, secondly provides targets that a sloth on Valium could achieve and finally as insurance is always 'work in progress'. The latter can be explained away as the need to be dynamic and proactive in a changing marketplace.

Marketing things to do

TV is the key medium if you can afford it, but if marketing budgets are tight the priority is to avoid cuts to salaries and expense accounts. So TV may have to make way for cheaper alternatives.

So it's back to the perennial favourite, print. For example, advertising in magazines or on posters or even 'direct mail'. This is the stuff that greets you on the doormat when you return home. There is a twin brother, the 'bill insert', which is the wad of paper, stuffed into an envelope that you need to get past to find your bill. Only the bored, the desperate, or the very lonely read this material. This segment of the population is ideal sales fodder for almost anything so it explains why this marketing method is relatively successful.

There are certain rules to follow for print advertising. Firstly the advertisement needs to have one of the following phrases in very big letters on the front.

FREE, 50% OFF, LAST CHANCE TO BUY, SPECIAL OFFER, MORE SEX

Introducing sex is always very successful but quite a difficult concept to work into an ad for tinned tomatoes. However, you don't need to because that's what an 'agency' is for.

The agency

The agency is the creative engine of the advertising world. Hives of pony-tailed, designer-suited, gaudily-shirted, trendy people and endless arguing about hues of purple and whether they are edgy or not. It's another world but wonderfully entertaining to experience.

One of the people you will work with is the account director, they will manage your project and spend your money. Also known as a 'suit', they have the drinking constitution of an ox and only eat at Michelin-starred restaurants. It's their job to pitch the idea to you and then get you to agree to the budget, which is always exorbitant, partly due to their expense account. The argument used will inevitably use the tactics of 'your product is so wonderful it deserves the best', or 'when your customers see this they'll buy it in bucket loads', or 'we're the best and that costs money'.

The implication being that if you don't agree to the costs, then your product will fail and it will be your fault. Of course, it's perfectly possible to spend the money and it will still fail but this will be blamed on 'changing market conditions' and not the campaign.

Bear in mind that the quote submitted and signed off by you is not the amount that you will actually fork out as it's about double that. The key to getting around the overspend is to get senior management involved at an early stage in the decision-making process. Every CEO is a frustrated creative and will spend hours deliberating over fonts, colours, scripts and all the unimportant bits. Inevitably this will result in a change of brief the night before the shoot. The mismatch between budget and the final invoice can then be blamed on this.

The brand identity

This used to be known as the corporate logo and long before that a sign. Now it is called the 'brand identity'.

In the good old days, a business communicated with its customers using signage. This prominently displayed the shop's name and trade, for example, 'Arkwright and Son: Grocer'. Which was handy because if you wanted some fruit and vegetables, in you went. Occasionally the message was reinforced by phrases such as 'Established since 1840' or 'By Royal Appointment'.

Nowadays companies call themselves thing like 'Thus' and 'Diageo' and it's much more confusing. This could have been solved by having logos that reflected the actual products or services provided by the business, but that is not currently in vogue either. Abstract is in. As a result, the prospective customer is often presented by an adverb and a squiggle, but may be comforted in knowing that this is 'modern, stylish and innovative'.

When considering a change in your corporate identity the following guidelines apply:

- The simpler the change, the larger the eventual cost
- 33% of the company will like the new logo, 33% will hate it and the others won't care
- The CEO's word is final

The last point is key. A wise MCA graduate will never express an opinion on any change to a brand identity. He will always slavishly follow the CEO's opinion. Of course, as soon as the logo starts appearing on the company notepaper you can claim full credit for having driven the creative process, suggesting the name and getting 'buy in' from the board. Remember everyone will be doing exactly the same so keep the specifics woolly when explaining your role in the process.

The campaign

All you really need to do is to tell the prospective customer what it is and how much it costs. If only it was that simple, nowadays the following guidelines must be applied:

- Everything has to be 'edgy' (including soft toys, which seems a bit dangerous)
- There needs to be a 'conversation' with the customer (even a BOGOF* one)
- 'Emotions' need to be 'engaged', even if you're selling toilet roll
- It has to reflect the brand 'DNA' (so it can presumably go viral)
- Companies must 'sweat' their brand assets (even if your stuff is 'cool')
- Consumers are always 'savvy' (hopefully not too savvy or they will buy your competitor's products, which are cheaper)

Customers

Customers are a necessary evil, you need them otherwise the pay cheques stop, but really they should be the sales

* Buy One Get One Free

team's responsibility so try and keep them at arm's length. Your PA should never transfer a customer's call to you; you should always be 'in a meeting'. It's all right to see them via a two-way mirror during a focus group, but make sure your exit is out the back of the building so there's no danger of actually meeting one, especially if they are 'savvy'.

Social media(crity)

And finally, social media. This is 'like' the most sweet 'like' marketing tool that has ever 'like' been invented, well bent and 'like' totally sick, no really, honestly mate. 'Like'.

Here are the basics for those that have no idea what I'm talking about.

First, however, you must employ someone either (if male) wearing a beanie hat, or (if female) has primary-colour highlights in her hair. They will also need a Mac laptop, as apparently social media doesn't work as well on a twenty-year-old office PC.

Social media has many forms, usually based on 'apps', which is 'software' you 'download' onto your 'device', which could be a 'smartphone' or a 'tablet'. You can then 'tweet', 'blog', 'pin' or 'like' stuff. Confused? Ask Beanie.

In an attempt to simplify this whole marketing nemesis, let's look at some of the marketing tools that Beanie uses and that you need to have a very high-level grasp of, just in case you meet someone important who is a lot younger than you.

Let's say your company makes widgets and you want

to publicise the fact to people who should really have read the paper, done some research, or at the very least read the leaflet you stuck through their door. Then you could use these social media apps:

SOCIAL MEDIA: WHAT DOES IT DO?

Twitter: I'm using my Widget now

Facebook: I like my Widget, do you?

LinkedIn: I made Widgets from 2010 – 2014

YouTube: Watch me play with my Widget

Pintrest: Here's lots of pictures of my Widget on holiday

Instagram: Look at my tinted Widget

Spotify: My Widget can whistle, listen here

Facetime: If you show me your Widget, I'll show you mine

Snapchat: Here's a picture of my Widget making a funny face

So there you have it. Simple. Beanie will 'upload' the correct 'media' to the right 'app' ensuring it has the correct 'format'. Just provide him with the information and it will be done as soon as he's finished the more urgent task of sorting out his yurt at the rave this weekend.

If you are feeling intimidated by all this, don't send any written or verbal communication about the information you need posted, just think about it. When it doesn't appear on your website, shout at him saying you used telepathy to communicate, and if he can't do it naturally, he should buy the bloody app.

Marketing Module

Are you 'edgy' or 'limp'?

Q1: The purpose of marketing is to:
A] Deliver compelling reasons for a customer to buy your product
B] Persuade people to buy something they don't necessarily need or want
C] Sell things
D] Fib in a believable way

Q2: A TV commercial is:
A] Expensive but ultimately a cost-effective way of getting your campaign across
B] Expensive
C] The TV bits that people fast forward
D] A chance to meet famous people and go on shoots in exotic locations

Q3: A marketing proposition could be:
A] A Unique Selling Proposition (USP)
B] A Customer Value Proposition (CVP)
C] A Compelling Researched Advertising Proposition (think about it)
D] The reason you got slapped at marketing's Xmas party

Q4: Research data can be delivered by:

A] Using qualitative or quantative methods

B] Interviews with focus groups

C] Using your intuition and unparalleled knowledge of the market

D] Using marketing-speak that is unintelligible to a normal person

Q5: The customer is always right:

A] Correct

B] Usually

C] Sometimes

D] Only if they agree with me

Answers

'The Best Module Ever' said 94% of persons recently asked in a qualitative survey conducted with a focus group. When asked what the right answers were they requested a further focus group session with a 2008 *Montrachet* rather than the *Rottvien* they had been served. These updated answers will be provided on our website in due course.

CHAPTER SEVEN

Strategy – Visions Without Medication

Strategy

This is one of the most important words you will ever use in your business career and it needs to be used often in front of your underlings, peers and bosses. Everything you do, from making a beverage to attending a staff meeting on the Christmas party, needs to have a strategic angle or a higher purpose that only you are aware of and forms part of the 'strategic plan' or 'strategic direction' for the company.

Tactical or operational plans imply 'doing' and that's not a good place to be as it also implies 'work' and 'accountability'. Of course, you will be allocated tasks by your manager, the more so if they are also MCA trained, but this simply means this task should be accepted and then delegated or passed on to another department.

So what is strategy?

A dictionary definition is:

> *A plan of action designed to achieve a long-term or overall aim.*

In a company it's at a lot higher level than that. Plans and actions are for workers and need facts and supporting evidence and research and forecasts, and the list goes on. This is very dull work and that's for the middle management to sort, not strategic thinkers with the 'helicopter view' of the 'big picture' where a grasp of detail is thought to be slightly suspect.

The current corporate governance model advocated by most large organisations today is based on the premise that senior management should create the strategy and the rest of the organisation should execute it. There are three major flaws in this idea:

- Senior management rarely has any idea on what the customer wants or needs
- They believe that they are generally much cleverer than the customer-facing staff who *do* know what the customer wants and needs
- There is an assumption that there are people available who can execute their brain dump, when in reality they are fully engaged developing last month's 'Big Idea for Growth'

Key Strategies

There are some important and very specific strategies that are well worth knowing about so that you can say them out loud in meetings to give the impression of being a serious player.

Cost leadership strategy

Now don't panic, this is not looking at reducing the cost of the leadership team. That would be foolish, as unless you pay outrageous sums you won't get the right people. Some cynics say that this is delivering an ever-upward spiral of salaries based on the fact that as soon as one group of CEOs gets a pay rise, the rest follow in order to ensure they are seen as the best in the market. Ridiculous!

Executive pay has risen in percentage terms faster than at any point in recent history despite the global downturns and panics of recent years. This is a good thing because as the crisis hit, our global business leaders got better and better because they had larger and larger salaries. And it follows that it must have been the less-well-paid CEOs that caused the issue in the first place.

So reducing leadership costs is not a good idea.

Cost leadership strategy is actually reducing the costs of producing your products to make them more competitive, so that you can sell them at lower prices but still make more profit. So the strategy here is: reduce costs at any cost.

This needs to be dressed up a bit and try not to put an auditable number at the end of the delivery period unless it's over five years away. You'll be long gone by then so it will be your successor's issue, not yours. Also remember the fall back for a quick win is a 10% downsize of the workforce and you can also significantly reduce the marketing budget, which is at least 50% wasted anyway.

Doing things differently strategy

Simply put, this is where you develop something that is unique or better than something that your competitors have. This is a good strategy because, in theory, you can charge what your want for this widget because, assuming it's what your customers want, then you can sell at a high price as no one else is selling one.

Of course, if your competitors are on the ball, quick on their feet and can spot an open goal, to use too many sporting analogies, then they'll make one themselves, only cheaper. And they haven't wasted zillions on R&D and they can hire your best people to make it with the money they've saved.

Luckily, most companies are mediocre like yours. By the time the suggestion has worked its way upwards through many levels of management and umpteen iterations of business cases and then been dismissed because the CEO didn't like the colour of the box it would be packaged in, the opportunity will have been missed.

This strategy, though, is rarely actually implemented, especially if you have a team of senior executives who are just constantly brimming with brand new ideas. They will happily bombard the development teams with 'can't fail' projects, which are low on detail and requirements, as they don't do that sort of thing. They also believe that execution is always a simple task, if the teams just applied themselves.

Typical ideas would be:

- A car with square wheels, which means it saves on brakes

- A perpetual-motion device
- A time machine
- An opportunity that you suggested six months ago that is re-packaged as theirs

Vision, Missions and Other Weird Stuff

A very long time ago, visions were had by medicine men, who were people who drank funny juice from the bark of the wonka wagger tree and then leapt about a bit, wearing silly hats whilst telling the tribe that the harvest was going to be good or bad, or that the Sun God was miffed about something. To retain a position of influence, the medicine man's vision statements did not upset the leader of the tribe, after all, he kept him fed and watered and provided a nice cave to live in. Generally speaking, very little of what they said was taken very seriously because it rarely came true, and anyway, it was entertaining to watch and filled an evening in front of the fire pit.

Today, not much has changed in the world of visions and although the presentation style has been updated a bit, it still requires some theatrics to entertain the shareholders and analysts.

Vision statements

A typical vision statement would be:

> *Global Widgets will maximise returns to our shareholders*
> *and deliver humongous profits by delivering world-class,*

innovative, high-quality widgets, punctually to all our customers at very competitive prices.

I've finished. You can wake up now.

A vision statement has to sound good to your customers, analysts and shareholders so they get a warm fuzzy feeling about your company when they read it. Any stated aims should have a timeline for delivery so far into the future that no one could be held accountable.

To create a vision statement is one of the most onerous tasks that the senior management will have to undertake. It may take up to a week to do and must always be undertaken in an environment that is conducive to creating an atmosphere where creativity and insight can thrive, away from the various distractions of the working day. A good place is a luxury resort on a Caribbean island.

Once the statement has been created it then needs to be communicated to the staff. It's obvious that as they are less insightful and do not have the big picture view that management have, many will not understand the message and may even scoff. But great works are often misunderstood in their lifetime and the company should plough on regardless. Most people can be bought off from outright revolt with a tee shirt with the message printed on it. After the vision statement comes the mission statement:

Mission statements

Mission statements originated from the military who

wrote down clearly what they were going to do, when they were going to do it and where it would take place. This is very important to get right when you have a lot of aggressive soldiers armed to the teeth with very dangerous and effective weaponry going off to kill people. Mistakes here due to misunderstandings are often very hard to rectify.

Nowadays, everyone from hairdressing salons to fairy cake manufacturers has to have a mission statement. Failure to apply the correct shampoo or not spreading enough icing is not quite as catastrophic as blowing up the wrong town, but it matters to these companies.

So to write a mission statement you need to identify what you want to do, how you'll measure that you've done it and how you will know it's finished. As an MCA student, alarm bells should now be ringing as this looks like:

- You may need to do something to achieve this
- You are publishing a measure you can be held accountable for
- There's a delivery date

So a typical mission statement might read:

To become the number-one fairy cake manufacturer in the country by selling the highest quality, freshest cakes, from factory to customer in under twenty-four hours on 80% of our range and with 99% customer satisfaction.

Now if the company knows that it takes thirty-six hours

to deliver 50% of their range and surveying customers would not provide a happy result, a rewrite is required so that it works in the real world:

> *To become the number-one fairy cake manufacturer in Cakesville★ by selling the highest quality, freshest cakes, from factory to customer in under a week on most of our range and with 100% customer satisfaction★★*

Sorted.

SWOT analysis

Strategies also require a bit of thought about why you are going to proceed down a particular path. The tool used is called a SWOT analysis and is the acronym for Strengths, Weaknesses, Opportunities and Threats. Many past and present junior execs will have done this exercise many times over to support suggestions to senior management. The analysis is designed to identify what's good about your company today (Strengths), what you could do in the future (Opportunities), what areas you are incompetent in (Weaknesses) and finally, what the world or your competition is about to do (Threats). The exec proposing an idea uses this to show why the proposed project or activity is a good thing, or how it prevents a bad thing. Either way it's a complex begging letter for funding.

★You are the only cake company in Cakesville
★★ Survey conducted post free beer/wine focus group, consisting of friends and family

However, beware. Filling in this matrix is fraught with danger for the naïve executive as the last thing you should point out in the CEO's current strategy is a weakness or your company's strength is based on a project that the board is just about to cancel.

Strengths
These are always derived from the company's vision or mission statement, or if the company doesn't have one, then derive this from the company's New Year message to the staff as this usually has a bit about what went well last year. Alternatively, use what will be told to the company's investors in a bid to get support for the remuneration committee's suggestion regarding board salary increases.

Weaknesses
Make sure these are always fluffy as specific issues could always be traced back to someone senior who is responsible for the problem. They will not forgive you.

If you are really clever, find something that isn't very good today but is just about to be fixed by someone you need to help further your career. Even cleverer, something that you have just fixed or will be fixed by an opportunity.

Opportunities
The projects that you need funding for, which cunningly also happens to resolve a weakness. Not too big a weakness or that will be thought of as criticising

management, and not too easy or the project may be taken away from you so someone else can take the credit.

Threats

They can be general, like a forecasted economic downturn, or inflation, or they can be specific, like a competitor's product. Only raise the latter if you can build something that at least looks like what they make.

Visions Module

Are you 'off your head' or 'out of your head'?

Q1: A vision:
A] Describes the high-level pathway to success for a company
B] Is management's productivity KPI
C] Can be translated into what was eventually achieved
D] Is the stunner in accounts

Q2: A SWOT analysis:
A] Identifies what's good and not so good about your company
B] Generally causes panic when written down
C] Can get rid of flies
D] Is a data intern doing the accounts

Q3: A mission statement:
A] Is a high-level objective that can be achieved
B] Means that you are a big company now
C] Is the output of a booze-fuelled executive jaunt
D] If not achieved, someone's gonna get liquidated

Q4: Strategic thinking is defined as:
A] Clear, big-picture goals to be delivered
B] Anything said by anyone on a VP or above grade

C] The stuff that clogs up day-to-day productivity

D] When read sounds cool, when spoken sounds silly

Q5: Which of the following strategic statements are true?

A] Money is not important; it's the challenge of the job

B] Exorbitant salaries retain the important people

C] Staff love mugs but only mugs love staff

D] Work is for those who can't manage

The answers can be found by holding the page up to the sunlight, if the outside temperature is at least 30°C. If by now you're not in an exotic location paid for by the company, we start to wonder if we are wasting our time here.

CHAPTER EIGHT

The CEO Zone

The CEO

The position of CEO or 'Chief Executive Officer' is the MCA graduate's ultimate goal. It's the top man, head honcho, big cheese and it carries a large salary, big stock options, over-generous pension contributions, plus a myriad of other financial and non-financial perks.

There's a fuel-guzzling car, possibly a chauffeur, and in the bigger companies, use of the company jet. Then there's first class travel, conferences in exotic places, fact-finding trips to the world's major cities, invitations to openings, first nights, restaurants, clubs, sporting events and so much more, plus free petrol, health care, dental care, lunches, dinners and golfing lessons. It's heaven on earth and any MCA graduate deserves it. So here is how to behave when you get the golden key to your personal executive washroom. Let's get your priorities right first.

Smile

Yes, that's right. CEOs smile a lot. The lower the ranks the more you smile at them. Whether handing out long-service awards or firing an entire division, just smile. This needs practice, it's not a 'grin' or a 'belly laugh', it's a confident smile with a faint aroma of arrogance and a hint of smugness. When you can do this, try a smile, then a fleeting 'cloud of concern look', followed by another smile. This brings a little more colour to your perceived persona.

The car

When you are promoted you will quickly need to get a new car. This shows everyone that change is uppermost in your mind and that things happen quickly. It's your first major visible decision and you need to get it right. The golden rule is that if you're under forty when you get the job, you need to purchase an executive saloon such as the top of the range Lexus, Range Rover, Mercedes or even a Bentley if you can get away with it. Avoid BMWs unless you've got a sales background. However, if you are older than forty you must get a two-seater sports car. This shows that you're young at heart, adventurous and up for anything. A Ferrari, Lamborghini, or similar, is the right type of brand here.

At this level you will have your own parking space at the front of the building. Ask for it to be spruced up a bit, as befits your position, with a potted plant or two, and get the white lines repainted. You should insist on a nameplate and get the letters done in gold paint. The security guard or post boy should be instructed to wash your car at least once a week. Make sure you pay them promptly, though, otherwise marks and scratches will mysteriously appear on the bodywork.

The office

The CEO's office is a statement of who and how powerful he or she is. The larger, therefore the better, ideally on the top floor with panoramic views of the surroundings. The higher up you are, the closer to God you appear to be. The office should also be a place of mystery. Invite only a select few in and then only to the conference table area. Juniors should always be made to stand, whilst senior managers can sit on a very small and hard chair, so that you can only see their head from your executive throne. All should be kept waiting outside for at least ten minutes and then inside for a while whilst you appear to be reading important confidential documents. It is also permissible to take calls at any time during these meetings. Any meetings should also be kept short and if you can manage to remain at your desk whilst the other attendees try to hold a meeting with each other, whilst straining around to see if you're listening or not, gives you an edge. Never hold any form of social occasion with staff or associates in here. It is permissible to have a high-ranking CEO from another company or a board member in for a drink at the end of the day. This is a particularly good wheeze to do on a Friday evening if you know one of the keener VPs is trying to get you to sign something. An hour or so cooling his heels in the waiting area will teach him not to bother you with these matters on a Friday, after all, you have got a home to go to.

The personal assistant

The PA should always be of the opposite sex. Therefore

if you're a male CEO, it's a 'she' and a female CEO, it's a 'he'. Your PA's most important role is to be the gateway to you. No one should speak to or phone you without having to go through this person. Remember, you are the CEO and anything you say will be done and that can be dangerous so it's better not to do too much communication.

Remember, it's a very personal relationship between CEOs and their assistants. They will run your diary, your life, your spouse's and children's lives and the day-to-day business of the company. This makes them very powerful and they know it. Never ever cheat on, damage the reputation of, or make a pass at your PA; the consequences are likely to be terrible. By all means be rude, late, difficult, demanding, irritable and even obnoxious occasionally is acceptable. This goes with the territory and is balanced out by the significant salary PAs are paid at this level. If the relationship is becoming rocky, a large present at Xmas usually smoothes things over. In a real crisis, purchase her/him a weekend at a luxury spa.

Communication

Anything you say will be taken as a key strategic input or even a vision; at the very least it's 'guidance'. Acolytes will hurry to write down these pearls of wisdom and will later convey them to their peers in hushed tones as though they had been written on biblical tablets of stone and handed down from a mountaintop. This can be fun, of course. It is always amusing to offer conflicting opinions on the same subject to rival VPs and wait to see what happens. This is best done on a Friday at around 6.00pm so that they both work a weekend to get a presentation ready for the Monday morning team meeting. You can award yourself double points if they both then present their different versions of the 'new strategy' at this meeting.

Of course, as a CEO you are not actually supposed to know anything, you hire people to do that for you. So never be specific with this 'guidance' but use phrases such as:

- 'Deliver improved shareholder value'
- 'Focus on the competition'
- 'Drive the bottom line'

These are fairly specific, so you can also use more general statements:

- 'I'm not happy with progress to date'
- 'Is this the best you can come up with?'
- 'Your colleague seems to grasp what I want'

This should send a shiver of fear through the hearer and should focus their minds on doing what you want them to do rather than plotting to get at you. By all means reward those who do your bidding without question, so you could send a quick email back along the lines of:

'I was interested to read your proposal and may discuss it with the board at a later date.'

Never say thank you or it will encourage staff to fill your mailbox with a myriad of other similar proposals.

Emails

As a CEO you will get hundreds of the pesky things from the workforce and it will seem every junior wants your attention and a decision. The former is irritating and the latter dangerous. The solution is filtering and the following methods can be applied:

- Don't answer, ever
- Get your PA to answer everything and then deny it was from you
- Answer with stock phrases like 'Noted', Why?', 'How much will this cost?' or 'Please reformat'

The simple question mark response is particularly effective:

? (Sows confusion)
?? (Sows consternation)
??! (Sows panic)

Decisions

It's a common fallacy that a key role of the CEO is to make decisions. Nothing should be further from your mind as it's the board's job to do this. Then if it goes wrong, and it often does, it's a collective responsibility and you can all pass the blame down the chain of command till you find a suitable scapegoat. Good decisions may be claimed personally after the event, but bear in mind that your fellow directors will also claim any credit.

On the board there will be more qualified people than you. There's a bean counter or accountant, the CFO (Chief Financial Officer). You'll recognise him as the one who always looks ten years older than he really is and talks in a dull monotone about market capitalisation and other financial gobbledygook. No need to get involved in this area unless he's obviously living beyond his means, then call the police.

The operations director is the one with his jacket across the back of his seat and wearing a short-sleeved shirt with coloured pens in the shirt pocket, again, avoid eye contact. He'll always volunteer for everything anyway.

There is also the marketing director. He'll be wearing clothes that are ten years too young for him and his hair will be coiffured with superglue. However, they always get invited to the best parties and events so keep on their right side. If succumbing to their charm and being forced into a decision-making position, always ask yourself whether you would buy a second-hand car off them. Then say no.

The four-year term and a five-year plan
All CEOs should follow the four-year management stint of a five-year business plan strategy. That is, you leave a year before completion and let the incoming CEO sort it out. All CEOs follow this practice so when you move

to another company you'll need to pick up the debris of the previous incumbent's plan. This is not a problem as you simply start up a new five-year plan. To the shareholders, anything will be better than the mess the company is currently in and you'll be seen as a beacon of change and they will grasp at any straws to save their investments.

A Day in the Life of a Typical CEO

07:30 Arrive in office. It's mandatory to arrive early, sorry. This is, however, the low point of the day. Fire over a few emails to underlings.

07:31 In conference (by yourself). Pull down blinds, instruct PA not to allow anyone in. Read paper and have quick doze.

08:59 Leave office and say to PA, 'Back in a minute.'

09:30 Return to office for 09:00 meeting.

09:35 Ask attendees for more data, new creative, another idea, etc. Wrap up meeting saying you have a 09:30 and imply it's their fault for not having achieved anything useful.

09:36 Pick up phone to your CEO friend at Trans-Global and discuss respective purchases of chalets at Swiss ski resort and do this with door open so assembled masses can hear.

10:00 Stick head around corner, ask PA to reschedule the 09:30 meeting for following month and close door. Continue on phone.

10:30 You need to get out and stretch your legs so go for a wander around the office. You'll need to be quick, though, as you're likely to get followed by a gaggle of anxious employees needing a decision or a signature or 'a quick word'. This exercise saves going to the gym and can really get the heart pumping. See if you can spot any slackers for later. Another neat trick is to walk unannounced into a meeting. If you do, just pick up on the first phrase you hear as you walk in and comment negatively on it. As the silence descends, say something wise like, 'Are you really focusing on the customer here?' Then leave. People will then admire your ability to pick up information quickly and get right to heart of the issue.

11:00 Safely back in the office, it's time to deal with pressing problems of the day, like investigating upgrading your car, a golfing holiday or a shooting weekend away with your mates.

12:00 Lunch – out of the office, of course, and on expenses.

14:00 In conference again – a quick snooze, or 'power nap' as it should more rightly be called.

16:00 Meeting – once a week you'll need to meet up for an hour or so with your direct reports. Ensure they follow the rules. Solutions not problems; good news out, bad news buried. Insist on a weekly detailed status report and when this is being presented, comment on the formatting rather than the content. Also leap ahead of the presenter and ask a question about slides three or four ahead of where he is. That will throw him off and in all likelihood he'll give a confused answer. Immediately patronise him with a 'This needs a bit more work, doesn't it?' type of statement.

16:30 Answer phone during meeting but insist the presentation carries on. It will look as though you can multi-task.

17:00 Summon any slacker you saw on your walkabout that morning. Ask them to provide a full proposal and business case for a project by 09:00 the following morning as you need to discuss it with the board.

18:00 Open emails again. Do not reply to anything that you don't understand or that costs money or has an attachment. Forward these on to one of your direct reports; ideally pick someone who you know has left for the day and demand a response ASAP.

18:05 Leave office. Leave light on, put jacket on back of chair and pull the blinds down so no one knows whether you have left or not. Get IT to sort the technology on your PC so it can send your answers to the emails hours after you've left the building.

23:00 Just before you go to bed, send short, pithy but unclear messages from your Blackberry to random direct reports containing 'guidance' and implying you may need to review a proposal tomorrow. Fall asleep to the imagined sounds of these people clicking away on their laptops far into the night creating presentations that will never be read.

Ah, power…

An MCA's relationship with the CEO

A quick look at the thesaurus provides the answer:

Servant, *attendant, domestic, drudge, helper, lackey, liegeman, maid, menial, retainer, skivvy, slave, varlet.*

An MCA should regard himself as an apprentice CEO, which is about as good as it can get in the self-belief stakes. Know your place, because a CEO does.

As this chapter implies, a CEO is a busy person. Not for him the drudge of day-to-day business, long hours and mental strain, but days filled with interfering, butt kicking, the settling of scores and a swagger or two around the office dispensing 'guidance'.

The MCA graduate who wishes to climb the greasy pole needs to be in attendance, or at least in view, during these office circuits. As CEO you will expect the MCA graduate to write down any pronouncement and communicate this throughout the business. The quid pro quo to this is that the MCA graduate will issue the dictum in a slightly different format. For example, if a CEO remarks that there seem to be a number of smokers huddling outside the back door, this will be translated into:

> *'I was chatting to Harvey during a steering board meeting where we were discussing the company's strategy related to smoking during work time. He was in complete agreement with my suggestion that this should cease forthwith and so will all supervisors ensure that this policy is communicated to the workforce.'*

For the CEO this is a win-win – productivity is increased and he didn't make the announcement.

A CEO's relationship with a VP

A VP wants your job so by all means hire someone bright as the company needs day-to-day management of the little people but don't hire anyone nicer than you. So long as they are complete and utter plonkers, then your position is safe. Communicating with VPs should be done by telepathy as this is by far the easiest form of corporate communication, but it is only possible to do if you're really senior. Corporate telepathy works on the principle that if you think it, it is transmitted. If the message is not picked up, then it is obviously the receiver's fault.

This doesn't work in reverse, though. If a VP transmits to a CEO, it's always on the wrong frequency and so VPs should not rely on this method to pass information back. Hence a VP's job is to anticipate any need and then make it happen.

A VP should also be able to detect if you're happy, sad, grumpy, irritable, or tired and should modify news, requests or information to suit your current mood.

The little people

Otherwise known as colleagues, associates, or in more traditional companies, the staff. They are the lifeblood of the company; the producers, the innovators, the number crunchers, the wealth generators and a whole lot of other epithets. Without them there's no company, no profits and no salary and no bonuses for you. So you need the little people, although not necessarily the ones you currently have, of course, and that's what keeps the equilibrium required to run a company.

By all means use the fear and greed principles because most people want an easy life supported by a monthly pay cheque. Remember, though, this is not a master-slave relationship or you end up with revolting staff and strikes and then your shareholders and non-execs get twitchy. Think 'remuneration committee' here.

Neither is it a father-son relationship, that's for small businesses only. It is much more akin to a dog owner's relationship with their pet. You feed and water them and throw sticks, they guard your house and pretend to like going after sticks. This relationship works, as the hierarchy is clear and everyone knows who's the boss, but it comes with some responsibilities and if both parties follow the rules, then harmony exists.

So when walking the shop floor, or talking at staff meetings, or attending Christmas parties, remember to smile, shake hands and look calm and collected, i.e. pet your pooch. That's what the little people want to see and what they expect. And their tails will wag.

The occasional chocolate drop and special treats will also work wonders and you will be rewarded with years of faithful servitude.

CEO Module

Will you be a 'big Dick' or a 'little Richard'?

Q1: To become a CEO you need:
A] Expertise, experience and energy
B] A big car, big house and a big ego
C] A plausible line in excuses for stockholders to get out of any scrape
D] Contacts

Q2: Your office has:
A] A door that is always open
B] A view across the city
C] Expensive artwork and pictures of you with famous people on show
D] Heard stuff that would make a Holy man despair for humanity

Q3: To raise middle management's performance:
A] Train, encourage and lead
B] Ignore their first three submissions of any request
C] Do the smile, frown, smile thing
D] A rocket up the proverbial always lifts standards

Q4: Customers:
A] Are the key focus of any business

B] Can be all right really, apart from the ones who complain all the time

C] Should be middle management's problem, not mine

D] Tend to impact on the efficiency of the operation

Q5: On my first day as CEO I will:

A] Meet with investors and analysts to discuss my vision

B] Meet with senior management to discuss strategy

C] Meet with the staff to discuss my plans for the company

D] Meet with my financial advisor to discuss tax havens

Answers

Obviously A is really the right answer in all cases and D is the worst answer.

However, if you are an A scorer, then your tenure as CEO will be short as you will quickly be overthrown by your 'colleagues' on the board. They think D is the right answer in all cases and if you want to stay as head honcho, then now you know what to do.

CHAPTER NINE

Presentations for Dummies

Nowadays it's almost impossible to avoid a meeting, a conference, or even some weddings without the ubiquitous power Microsoft PowerPoint or similar slide presentation. For anyone who doesn't know PowerPoint, it's software that projects an electronic slide onto the screen or a wall. This slide can then be filled with text, graphs, pictures or almost anything that prevents the audience looking at the presenter. This means that the presenter can waffle, tug at his flies, tweak their locks, and jangle their keys or almost any of the one hundred things you're not supposed to do when presenting to an audience. Overnight, we all became adequate presenters.

These presentations are now often called 'packs' or 'decks'. In many companies, and all those run by ex- or actual management consultants, the formatting of the slides will determine whether or not it's read.

Hot tip for those working for consultants: If you need to produce a presentation overnight and therefore have to cancel a night out, then write any old thing down but use an old template. Your presentation will be hurled back at you unread at 09:01 the next morning to be reformatted, which will give you an extra day to produce the work.

Types of Presentation

The usual reason for creating a slide presentation is to communicate lots of information to an audience. For health and safety reasons this audience is almost always seated so they don't fall over from boredom and hurt themselves. The number of slides in the presentation is inversely proportional to the seniority of the deliverer. The more senior you are, the less slides you have.

The senior management presentation

This is the least slide heavy. There are only a handful of slides and a lot of them are pictures of happy staff or gleaming products. Facts are kept to a bare minimum meaning less likelihood of difficult questions or bad press. Rarely created by the manager concerned, it's often glossy but has the intellectual depth of a stagnant pool in a drought.

You may use the presentation at the top of the next page as a template (just change the company name/logo, etc.) as it is relevant to most mediocre companies.

First introduce yourself and tell a joke. A bit of self-deprecation helps, for example:

> *Someone asked if I knew a good plastic surgeon. Would I look like this if I did?*

But emphatically not:

> *Someone asked if I knew a good CEO. Would I be in charge if I did?*

The audience will now be in the palm of your hand.

Now comes the presentation body itself. A senior manager should ask themselves the following questions:

- Is my company doing everything legally, transparently and effectively?
- Does everyone in this audience respect, admire and like me?
- Am I certain that any company problems cannot be traced back to me?

If the answer is 'yes' to all three questions, skip this chapter. If not, read on.

The first slide is always the strategic one, generically dull but with the usual underlying messages.

The Helicopter View

- **Delivering Shareholder value**
  (Fired more than I hired this year)

- **Delighting our Customers**
  (Most went to our competitor and they seem happy now)

- **Exceeding Market Expectations**
  (Wasn't quite as bad as everyone thought it was going to be]

Delivering...

Competitive

Reliable

Advanced

Products

NB. The underlying slide messages are in italics.

Of course, there's no need to read any of this out, even exec SVPs have literacy to this level.

Just use the time available to drop some names of VIPs who you've met or are about to meet and how supportive they have been. And then follow up with an anecdote that starts, 'I was skiing with the minister last week...'

Also note how many people are:

a] *Asleep*
b] *On their smartphones doing emails*
c] *Paying attention*

Don't worry about the first two as they are harmless. It is the ones who are taking notes who might cause problems by asking questions at the end. They could be consultants, or worse, journalists. Fire off a couple more

'Look at me, I'm great' anecdotes that should soon convince them to join groups a) or b).

So keep it short, keep it simple. As you can see the idea is to radiate generalities rather than specifics but couched in the language your audience will understand. The acid test is to imagine one of these statements as a headline in the business section of a newspaper. Will it come back to haunt you? For example, saying: 'A 50% increase in profits is forecast for this year' might well do that, so never put that on a slide.

Our Strategic Focus

• **A clear Vision set the culture and tone**
 [Made a few threats, shouted a lot and got my own way]

• **Thought-through Objectives drove the policies**
 [Me to get rich very quick]

• **Dedicated and loyal Leadership Team**
 [Soon be replaced by a more toadying sycophantic set]

Delivering...
Competitive
Reliable
Advanced
Products

When presenting, dress casually but expensively and occasionally look at an imaginary person at the back of the room and acknowledge them with a nod, to imply you know lots of important people. Each company will have slight variations on how these slides are specifically phrased but it's a very useful way of going public with a show of strength underpinned by general threats before doing this with your team in private. 'Stay mean and keep them keen.' Remember, at some point a senior manager will not be able to rut effectively anymore and will be metaphorically chased out of the boardroom plain to the wilderness of the golf club.

Solid Deliverables

• **We will reward Success**
[*share options, enhanced pension contributions, big bonuses*]

• **We will run an Efficient organisation**
[*downsize and re-organise to pay for point 1*]

• **We will Plan for the future**
Will line up a new job for 4 years time when I introduce the 5 year plan

Delivering...
Competitive
Reliable
Advanced
Products

Finish off with an upbeat message that looks ahead to a rosy future under your command. At the end of the presentation shake the hands of a rival CEO and pretend you're really good mates. Then walk out. You're far too busy to listen to anyone else's presentation and anyway, they are not going to tell you anything you don't already know.

The basic MCA presentation

Many courses and books on presentation technique suggest you open with an anecdote, then tell them what you're going to say, say it and then summarise at the end. But you'll need to turn this into a career-enhancing move.

After all, you're in front of an audience that can be divided into placings on the corporate ladder.

a] *Lower down (not important)*
b] *Same level (potential competition)*
c] *Higher up (promotion or next job opportunity)*

So the anecdote should be based on how you saved the company, came up with the new idea, or made the first million sales. It doesn't have to be completely true, just giving the story enough facts to make it seem plausible. By the end of the presentation they will have forgotten the detail.

Next, launch into the presentation. If you can get all your three-pointer slides to state the obvious in pure business clichés, then you're well on the way to MCA presentation glory. Remember, most of your audience doesn't want to be there, they have better things to do than attend this conference or meeting and thus being 'out of office' could result in actions being handed out, or fingers pointed, or a whole host of other activities that could directly impinge negatively on their day. So make it innocuous, safe and flaccid so they can doze off. You know you're really safe from scrutiny if you can count at least ten people on their Blackberries answering emails.

This is particularly important if presenting at a conference abroad. Half will have overdone it the night before, so the last thing they need is strenuous mental exercise. The other half are consultants who earn their pay cheque by regurgitating facts and figures they note down at conferences like these. Some of the younger, less experienced ones take notes and then ask clever questions at the end of your presentation. Gently remind them afterwards, at networking drinks, that their company will now not be welcome to pitch for business.

Your MCA-style presentation should always include the following topics:

- Sales
- Strategy
- Marketing

But remember, include data but no facts.

1: Increased sales

This demonstrates that before you arrived the situation was grim, but today it's getting better and in the future it will be wonderful. Remember, though, the future never has a date attached so you don't actually have to deliver.

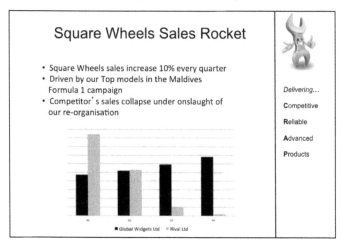

Obviously in your world, sales always go up and costs come down. In the chart above it looks like your company is not only doing very well, as sales are obviously increasing, but also, Rival Ltd, your main competitor in the wheel market, has sales figures that seem to have imploded. And this can all be attributed to your marketing campaign and reorganisation.

The fact that Rival Ltd stopped making their square wheel at the start of the year to concentrate on the development of a round wheel is not mentioned. Next year's chart will not feature square wheel sales, though. Remember, you don't want to put any values on any of the segments, this is, of course, 'confidential', but you can wave vaguely at the screen and get the audience to appreciate that the darker bits are bigger than the lighter bits and that's obviously a good thing. So never include actual facts, they just get in the way of your story.

2: Strategy

This is always a complicated slide, harder to understand and copy down, and shows that Global Widget Ltd is the market leader, doing better than its competitors and knows where it is going.

It's important again not to give away any information that could be checked. For example, in this slide note the use of Afghan, Bulgarian and Zimbabwean currencies for the different financial metrics. The profit, of course, is always stated in the local currency.

The SWOT analysis highlights all the key advantages but should be circumspect about any disadvantages. And

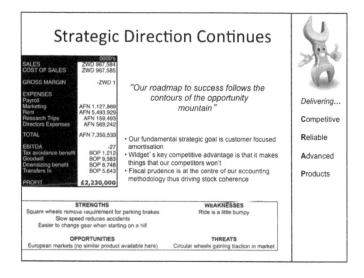

finally, strategic statements should be vague and woolly so that at the next investors' meeting it can be confidently stated that they were all achieved.

3: Marketing presentation

Marketing has been covered in greater detail elsewhere on this course but even if you are not intending to become a marketing professional, because you are qualified to do a proper job, you should be able to communicate marketing things effectively.

The key to understanding this presentation is that although there are marketing 'messages' these are delivered as a 'conversation' As with most conversations, one person does the talking whilst the other pretends to listen but is really trying to get a word in.

So marketing plans, campaigns, promotions, etc. do

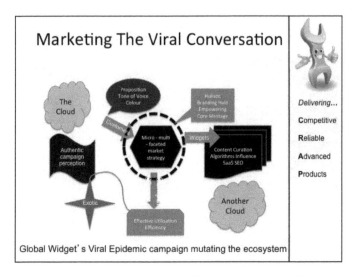

not actually have to mean anything, they simply have to sound important and need a lot of lunches to get the 'tone of voice' right.

As you can see in the slide, there are a lot a shapes and arrows and this is important as it shows the interconnected-ness of all activities and the synergy between a widget and the known multiverse, most major religions and cute, fluffy, baby animals.

Don't forget to bring in terms like SEO (Search Engine Optimisation) where by spending a vast amount of your company's marketing budget on entertaining and agency trips to spas in exotic locations, you can increase visits to your website by 500% or more. This will justify your expense account when the CEO has to sign it off. The fact that your website went from five views to twenty-five views per month should not be highlighted in this instance.

Presentation Module

Ensuring the information super-highway meets the roadworks of corporate jargon.

Q1: Effective communication is:

A] A key tool to ensure the staff know what's going on

B] A problem because the staff will then know what's going on

C] Muddling the message so no pointy fingers later

D] Shouting loudly

Q2: A presentation is used when:

A] Important information needs to be disseminated to a large number of people

B] It gets you free flights and entry into an international conference as a speaker

C] You need to impress someone but need some visual clues about what you're talking about

D] The issue is better confused than clarified

Q3: The optimum number of slides for a thirty-minute presentation are:

A] Less than ten, so there's time to talk round the key points

B] The same number as the generic presentation you always use

C] At least thirty so you can whip through the facts before anyone copies them down

D] The same number as my claimed achievements can be stretched out to

Q4: Presentations can be made more effective by:

A] Using text, images and graphs to highlight points and metrics

B] Not reading out every single word written on the slide behind you

C] Reading out every single word written on the slide behind you

D] Using a laser pointer and occasionally shining it on the centre of the forehead of someone doing emails

Q5: Your presentation is wiped five minutes before you go on stage, do you:

A] Carry on, you have a spare copy on a USB

B] Carry on and wing it, you know your stuff and you've been practising

C] Ask to be dropped down the order and get a copy emailed over from the office

D] Use the next speaker's presentation and watch his face as the horror begins to dawn

Answers

So you're getting the hang of these modules now. Mostly Ds will get you a pass here. For bonus marks please submit a three-slide 'deck' that could be used either by the marketing director of a toad sexing company, or by a process engineer who makes cherry-flavoured frankfurters. The topic is Authentic Awareness Alignment.

CHAPTER TEN

Jargonization

In this final chapter you will now learn how to communicate effectively in the world of business. The whole point being to convince your underlings, peers and paymasters that, for example:

> *'Moving forward we can drive the roadmap deliverables by utilising exploratory research pointers and thus facilitating the company's strategic processing paradigm strategy.'*

If you do not understand what this means, fear not, no one else does either and so you will never be held to account if nothing very much happens in this area, wherever that area is.

The world of business communication is now so complex that it is likely that there will soon be a formal modern language course in the subject. Top universities will offer 'Business Jargon' as an honours degree for the aspiring business nerd. Yummy mummies will be taking Arthur and Agnes to pre-school classes in 'Daddy-speak'. Conservative education ministers will have classloads of year sevens chanting 'Run it up the flagpole and see if the cat's sick' by rote. So you really need to get ahead of the game here. If you have followed the text so far, then you will have noticed a number of incomprehensible phrases have crept in, so if you got through that, then you are already on your way.

A word of caution here, do not try to use this language in a domestic situation. For example, asking a friend to 'consider a beverage-focused objective within an alcohol-centric platform' rather than just suggesting you go to a pub, will get a blank stare.

Let's looks at the definition of Business Jargon (BJ).

> *Business jargon is used to explain an activity or action by seeking to create the impression that the generator of the message possesses a high level of sophistication, skill and business knowledge. Business jargon is characterised by its use of buzzwords, inaccurate or irrelevant metaphors and terms appropriated from unconnected fields, such as sports or the military, that create almost meaningless messages.*

Perfect. Confusing the message and giving out meaningless information is the object here. Unless you work in bomb disposal, when clarity really is key.

The importance of BJ to a company can be gauged by checking if it claims to have 'corporate values'. As obviously as a corporation is an entity and not a person, it cannot therefore have 'values'. But if it thinks it does, then BJ is the language that will be used internally. Curiously, though, the majority of employees, when asked, will claim that they despise BJ but will then 'convene a thought shower to bring to the table alternative win-win scenarios to replace business jargon'. But BJ has its uses, as using this language can hide very unpleasant things. Even the most hardened manager wants to be loved a little, so it's a lot easier to dress up firing someone or making them redundant as 'downsizing' or 'smartsizing'. And, of course, obfuscating anything, with business jargon, allows room for error and therefore avoids being blamed so keeps you out of the 'downsizing' pool. Win-win again. So never call a spade a spade because it just might not be to your boss.

Top ten business jargon phrases

1] **Outside the box:** When you have an idea, it's obviously cleverer than anyone else's so it's outside their narrow container of corporate thinking.

2] **Blue sky thinking:** A formal way of saying the first thing that came into your mind when asked to contribute in a meeting.

3] **Run it up the flagpole:** When someone else has a good idea and raises it, it's a chance for everyone to pull it to pieces.

4] **Thought shower:** Used to be known as 'brainstorming'. When everyone sits in a room in silence until someone senior suggests an idea and then everyone agrees with it.

5] **Level playing field:** Everyone is equal but some managers, like you for example, are more equal than others (to paraphrase George Orwell).

6] **Paradigm shift:** Any change by you is a paradigm shift and is therefore groundbreaking. Anyone else's change is either business as usual or they've totally lost the plot.

7] **Cutting edge:** It's new, it's different, it's edgy. The only way you can explain this is to 'blog' about it, so well done you!

8] **Action it:** What the little people do. Note that nothing is impossible if you don't have to do it yourself.

9] **Moving forward:** After any disaster that can be traced back to you, you look the accuser in the eye and say 'Let's just move forward', implying that they are now the one with issues.

10] **Roadmap:** At the beginning of the year you need a document that justifies why you need more staff and more budget. Unlike an actual roadmap, it is not based on reality but on perception. If you used a business roadmap to get from A to B you would arrive at Z, a year late, via a roller coaster and an unmarked minefield.

So as you can see, the rule is to generate a business or personal advantage by creating confusion through baffling terminology.

Appraisals jargon

These are the annual meetings where the appraisee (getting the appraisal) wildly exaggerates last year's work in the hope of getting a pay rise, whereby the appraisor (doing the appraisal) is tasked by management to refuse pay rises and where possible, reduce headcount. Business jargon is again important to ensure both sides think they got what they wanted.

Usually the appraisee has to fill in a form explaining what was done, how well it was done and whether it was done on time and on budget. Inevitably there is confusion when the data submitted by the appraisee is compared to the actual truth. However, as it can usually be shown that at least 80% of the barriers to achieving the set objectives were clearly caused by reorganisations, budget cuts and changed priorities, often actioned by the appraisor, it's not that simple to resolve. Inevitably the meeting will overrun and get fractious. Compromise is the order of the day and both parties leave the meeting feeling a little soiled but grateful it's over for another year.

When writing up the appraisal, the manager must be careful to ensure that nothing is said that could come back to haunt the company should the employee get the hump and decide to sue for mismanagement.

The following terms may be used in an appraisal report, which will be understood by HR but not by the employee.

Top ten HR terms
1] **Average** (thick as two short planks)
2] **Active socially** (drinks too much)
3] **Strict disciplinarian** (a bastard)
4] **A good judge of people** (has favourites)

5] Takes advantage of opportunities to progress (buys drinks for bosses)

6] Finds logical solutions to problems (gets someone else to do it)

7] Stays late to finish work (no friends or home life)

8] Conscientious and careful (scared of making mistakes)

9] Demonstrates leadership qualities (shouts a lot)

10]Principled and focused (stubborn)

Consultancy jargon

At some point in your career you may have reason to employ consultants and therefore you will need to know how to communicate with one. The old adage that a consultant is someone who borrows your watch and then tells you the time is very true, except that if they just said 'It's ten past three', then you are not going to pay them as much as if they said:

> *Based on a quantum logic clock rather than an aluminum ion clock, which only has a measured frequency to the current standard of 1121015393207857.4 Hz, we can confidently tell you that, going forward, at the same precise time twenty-four hours ahead, neither gaining nor losing one second in 3.7 billion years, the time will still be 15:10.*

The result is still the same but you're now happy to shell out thousands for that insightful and thought-out piece of work that seemed simple at first but was obviously far more complicated than envisaged. So it's important to be able to understand the terminology and so if you are paying well over the odds, then you can at least explain the expenditure to your boss.

The following consultancy terms are key to making the simple, complex, the obvious, confused and the fees, exorbitant.

Top ten consultancy terms

1] Helicopter view: The high-level view, the big picture, i.e. lots of noise and you feel sick.

2] Leverage: Using a metaphorical wedge to get into the CEO's office to complain about the staff who are being rude about you.

3] Move up the value chain: Charging more for your services as you get more experienced.

4] Outsourcing: Downsizing the people who moaned about you asking them what they did all day.

5] Quick win: Identifying a key research meeting with a company situated in a ski resort.

6] Bang for your buck: What rabbits do when they want little rabbits.

7] Ping: Responding to an email sent to you by the person sitting at the next desk by flicking a rubber band at their ear.

8] Low-hanging fruit: After weeks of creating slide decks, proposals and strategy papers, the point where the idea suggested months ago by the boss's PA seems to be the only viable option.

9] Sweating the assets: The feeling on Monday

morning after a couple of kegs of lager followed by an extra spicy vindaloo on the weekend.

10]**Deep dive:** If the boss appears on a Friday evening looking for a volunteer to provide a detailed analysis of a proposed deal to be on his desk Monday morning, then a deep dive underneath your desk should keep you out of the line of sight.

The other benefit of learning BJ is that it is a universal language so no need to learn French or German or even Chinese to get ahead in the global economy. This type of commercial claptrap has gone viral and is spoken everywhere. So now go confidently forward, driving best practices, utilising available bandwidth as you bring to the table a business model that will get buy in.

Jargon Module

Definitize the quasi-documented terminological letter sets below:

Q1: A critical path:
A] An important bit of a roadmap
B] The bit that delays everything else
C] The walk to the boss's office on your way to being told off
D] Best avoided so go round the long way

Q2: Peel the onion:
A] Lifting the stone to see what's crawling underneath
B] Part of the implementation process when constructing a salad
C] Slightly less pointless task than peeling a grape
D] Makes you cry when you see what's underneath

Q3: World class:
A] No one does it better than me
B] Quite good
C] Better than flying first class
D] Your ability to sink alcohol after a hard week at the office

Q4: Touch base:

A] Meeting someone also wearing a suit

B] An American sporting term used in baseball

C] Do this metaphorically, not physically, if you want to avoid a slap

D] Call me urgently, I need something from you

Q5: Wetware:

A] A human solution

B] An anorak

C] Being afraid of swimming pools

D] Spilling a mug of coffee into your laptop

Answers

Please drill down your final metrics and disintermediate any de-scoped results, then circle back around with the turnkey solutions.

Conclusion

You have now completed the Master of Corporate Administration course.

Your academic studies now need to be consolidated by some practical projects to ensure the information is fully embedded in the back-end lobe of your brain. This is the primaeval part where the base instincts of greed and self-preservation are based and now need to be trained to dominate the softer parts, which manage compassion, love and general wimpyness.

Activities to practise

[1] Shouting to get your way. Start with an inanimate object such as a chair, then build up via small furry animals till you feel confident enough to use on a low-ranking colleague.

[2] Create a hypothetical sixty-slide business plan using only business jargon and submit to the board and then see if this is adopted as 'worthy of further investigation'.

[3]   Delegate every alternate allocated action sent via email to random people in the company, suggesting that 'this looks exactly like the challenge you should get your teeth into'. If there is any pushback say, '[insert MD's first name here] suggested you were the right person'.

Congratulations you can now join the famous alumni who have also graduated and now lead most of the world's most mediocre companies.

Never let the b*gg*rs get you down!

Dick Lannister
MCA *Summa Cum Laude*